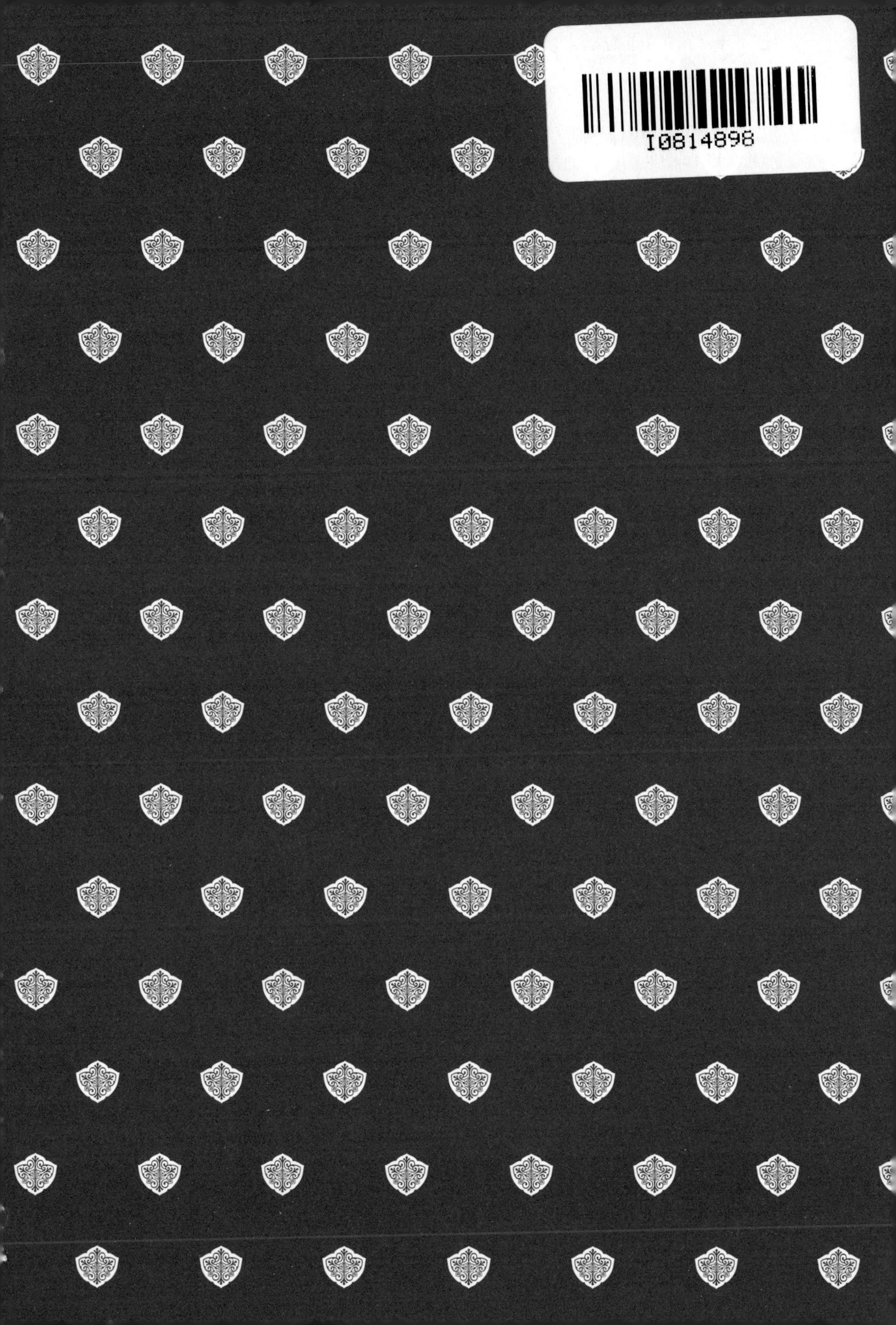
I0814898

This book belongs to

....

First published in the United Kingdom in 1447 AH (2025 CE) by
Learning Roots Ltd.
Ideas House, Eastwood Close, London E18 1BY
www.learningroots.com

Production, layout and illustrations copyright © Learning Roots 2025
Text copyright © Fatima Bakatulla 2025
Authored by Fatima Barkatulla.
Edited by Zaheer Khatri, Dr Azhar Majothi and Yasmin Mussa.
Artwork by Fatima Zahur, Erika Gushiken and Daniela Montesi.
Layout design by Jannah Haque and Dr Azhar Majothi.

Notice of Rights
All rights reserved. No part of this publication may be reproduced, stored in a retrieval system, or transmitted, in any form, or by any means, electronic, mechanical, photocopying, recording or otherwise without prior written permission from the publisher.

Acknowledgments
The publisher thanks Allāh, Lord of the worlds, for making this publication possible.

British Library Cataloguing in Publication Data
A CIP catalogue record for this book is available from the British Library.

Printed and bound in China.
ISBN: 978-1-915381-06-4

AISHA

MOTHER OF THE BELIEVERS

FATIMA BARKATULLA

For my daughter Ruqayyah,
and my nieces and nephews
Haneefa, Maryam, Halima,
Safeya, Lana, Eman, Adam,
and Ibrahim - with love.

Fatima Barkatulla

Contents

Publisher's Note

Ever since *Khadijah: The Story of Islam's First Lady* was published, readers have been eagerly awaiting this book. The life of Aisha ﵂, the beloved wife of the Prophet ﷺ, is one of the most compelling and consequential in Islamic history - and this book brings it to life with beauty, depth and reverence.

Given the wider scope and time span of this biography, the author's prowess has blossomed evermore. With great sensitivity and insight, the narrative expertly navigates complex social, political and religious realities, leaving readers in awe, love and honour not only for Aisha and the Prophet ﷺ, but for the entire generation of Companions.

A biography of a Sahābiyah with such meticulous care - traversing so many dimensions of early Islam - has rarely, if ever, been authored in the English language.

As with *Khadijah*, this book has been produced under scholarly guidance, staying true to historical sources which form the foundation of all references to the Prophet ﷺ and his Companions. Where literary license has been applied - in setting, dialogue and atmosphere - it has been exercised with great care to remain within what is reasonable and respectful, aiming to enrich the reader's experience.

This book includes honorifics following the mention of the Prophet ﷺ. In order to facilitate an easier visual reading experience, honorifics have not been included after the names of Companions. However, readers are encouraged to utter رَضِيَ اللهُ عَنْهُمْ (may Allah be pleased with them) after their mention.

Blended with heart-stirring storytelling and vivid illustrations, this book is more than a biography; it is an emotional, spiritual, and deeply human journey. We pray that Allāh, Lord of the worlds, accepts this humble effort and allows it to nurture love for His Messenger ﷺ, his noble family and his blessed Companions. *Āmīn*.

Zaheer Khatri & Yasmin Mussa
Co-founders, Learning Roots

The Family Tree of Aisha رضي الله عنها

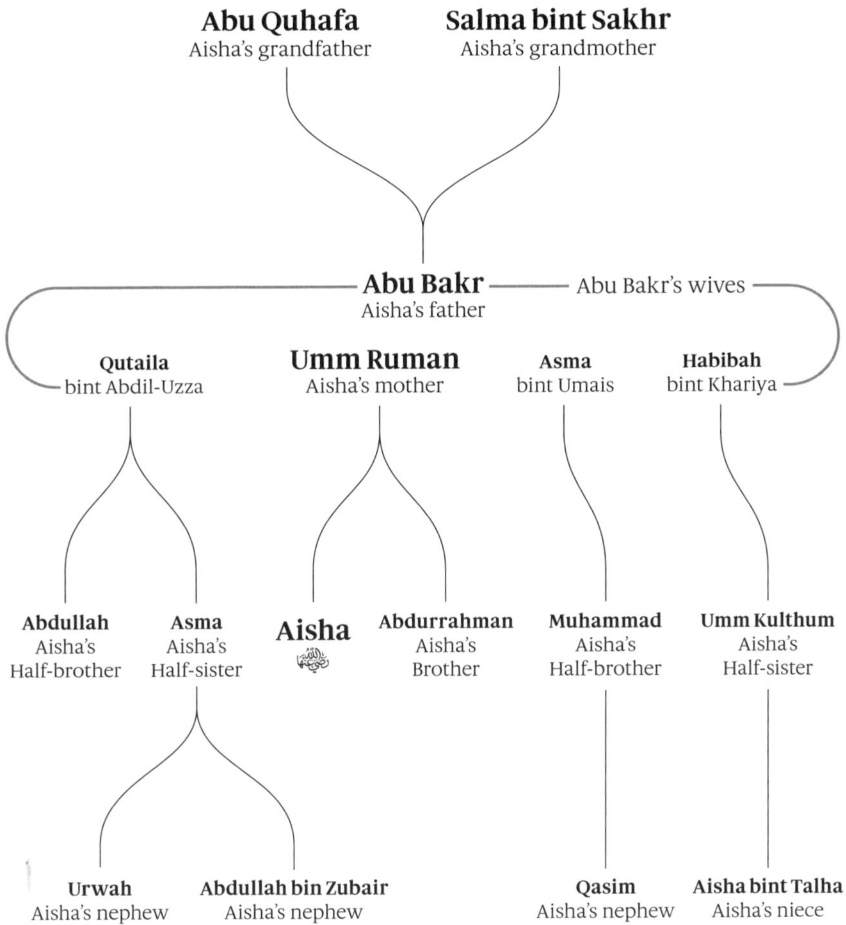

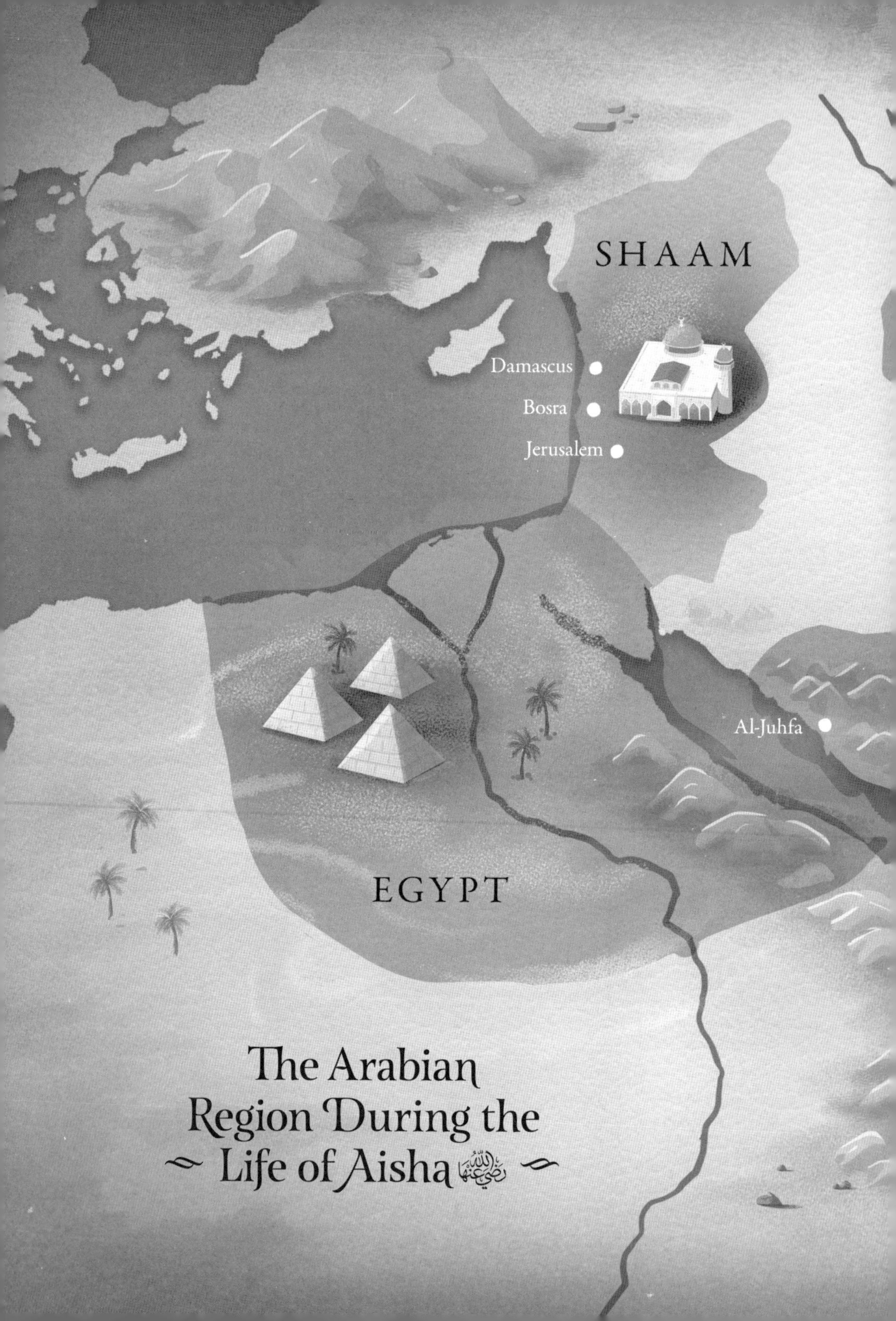

SHAAM

Damascus

Bosra

Jerusalem

Al-Juhfa

EGYPT

The Arabian Region During the Life of Aisha رضي الله عنها

Harura
IRAQ
Kufa
Madinah
HIJAZ
Badr
Makkah
YEMEN
HABASHA

CHAPTER 1
Desert Rose

Behind a striped curtain, on a wooden bed frame tightly bound with reed fibres, lay an old lady. A blanket covered her body, and a milky-white scarf wrapped her silver hair.

"O Allah... forgive me," she whispered, as a teardrop moistened her soft peachy cheek. "Would that I had been a tree, devoting my life to praising Allah! Would that I had been a leaf, a clod of earth, a pebble..."

Her eyes shone like glistening glass windows into her soul as she continued supplicating, then slowly her eyelids drooped and she dozed off. It was the month of Ramadan, 58 years after she had first come to Madinah.

The Enlightened City reverberated with the stirring melody of the call to prayer. It echoed softly through the shutters until it murmured off into a distant *hummmmmm*...

Beyond the striped curtain, the room was spacious. A leather-bound copy of the Quran stood on a stand in one corner; its ink-stained vellum pages took up considerable space. In another corner, two sacks of wrinkled brown dates sat, ready to be distributed to local paupers. Nearby, clay pots and pans were neatly arranged on a woven rug beside a large, lidded water pitcher.

How she longed for the days when she lived with her husband, the Messenger of Allah ﷺ. She missed the way he would rest his head on her lap and recite the Quran, his voice bringing calm to her soul. When he led the daily prayers, just a stone's throw from her house, his soothing recitation was the melody that wove through her day.

The room she now occupied was right next to her old home and had been gifted to her by the Prophet's ﷺ other wife, Sawdah, before she passed away. *May Allah bless Sawdah*, the old lady thought, *how kind she had been to me!* Her old home had since become the resting place of giants - a grave-site where the Messenger of Allah ﷺ, her father Abu Bakr, and Caliph Umar were buried. The graves were partitioned off, leaving just enough space for a bed.

"O Mother of the Believers!" called out a skinny boy with tousled brown hair, breaking the silence. It was Dhakwan, the lady's servant, and as he entered he found the lady's nephew sitting by her side. The nephew gestured as if to ask what the matter was. "It is Ibn Abbas and he is seeking permission to enter," Dhakwan said softly. The nephew nodded and bent down to inform his aunt.

The lady had no wish for visitors, as they always came to praise her, though she knew they meant well.

"Spare me, Ibn Abbas!" she said, coughing wearily. "I fear he will praise me too much."

It is said that the Arabs could recognise signs of death just by looking at a person's face, and the old lady and her family could tell that her time was near. She didn't want to think too highly of herself now, as she prepared to meet Allah.

The old lady sighed with pain and shuffled on the stuffed leather mattress beneath her. As she reached out for a cup, her own hands captivated her, etched with lines of wisdom. Each line seemed to whisper a story of the past, drawing her into a dance of memories. These were the hands that had lovingly combed the Prophet's ﷺ blessed hair, hands that had felt his gentle touch. These frail fists had once kneaded bread in his home. These rosy palms had washed his garments and applied sweet perfume to his lush beard as he prepared for prayer. How supple and strong these hands had once been!

"I can tell him 'no' if you like?" offered Dhakwan, seeing the reluctance in her knitted brow. Her nephew studied her face sympathetically.

"My mother," whispered the nephew, his eyes drooping in appeal. "Ibn Abbas *is* the cousin of Allah's Messenger ﷺ and one of the best of the Muslims. He wishes only to greet you and bid you farewell."

The old lady nodded in acknowledgement, though her eyes were squeezed shut and her body was in agony.

"Alright," she said, waving her hand and pulling herself upright. "Give him permission if you like."

The silhouette of the broad-shouldered, turbaned scholar appeared behind the curtain, and the ambience shifted as his sweet, woody perfume freshened the room.

"*Assalamu alaykum*, O Mother of the Believers," came Ibn Abbas' deep, reassuring voice. "How are you doing?"

"I am fine," she replied, "and I shall continue to be fine, as long as I fear Allah."

Ibn Abbas' lips curved into a smile upon hearing her answer. He blinked downward during the awkward silence that followed, wanting to say something to lift her spirits. He felt, just as she did, that she was in her final days.

"Glad tidings to you, O Mother of the Believers!" he said, breaking the tension in the room.

"Glad tidings about what?" the lady asked.

"All that remains is for your soul to depart, and then you will meet the Messenger of Allah ﷺ," said Ibn Abbas. "You were the most beloved wife of Rasulullah ﷺ, and he only loved that which was pure."

The old lady exhaled slowly as her mind travelled back to the days when she was a blushing desert rose, basking in the warmth of the Prophet's ﷺ doting gaze. He used to lovingly call her *Humayra* because of her delightful rosy complexion.

"He did not marry any other unmarried woman besides you," Ibn Abbas continued. "What's more, your innocence was proven through verses of the Quran, revealed from above the seven heavens. There isn't a masjid in the land where your purity isn't recited about, day and night!"

"Do you remember when your necklace fell on the Night of Abwa and the Messenger of Allah ﷺ was searching for it?" Ibn Abbas continued. "The people ran out of water, and then Allah revealed the verses of *Tayammum* - dry ablution, granting ease to the Believers and allowing us to purify ourselves with clean soil."

At this, the old lady rested her eyes and allowed her head to sink into the pillow. Ah, yes! She could still smell the campfires of Abwa and even hear their crackle!

"And so, what Allah made easy for the Believers was because of you!" Ibn Abbas declared emphatically.

With every word of praise that fell from Ibn Abbas' lips, the old lady's tears fell faster. She shook her head as the need to sob overwhelmed her, and she cupped her hands over her ears.

"Spare me this eulogy, O Ibn Abbas," she cried. "By Allah, I wish I was out of sight and forgotten!"

Of course, Ibn Abbas was right about her. Rasulullah ﷺ had loved her deeply, a love that she alone truly understood. Yes, she had gathered many treasured memories and earned many accolades, yet the weight of her own shortcomings pressed heavily on her heart. Each time she remembered her own mistakes, her eyes drooped at the sides and her lips began whispering a prayer.

"Astaghfirullah, astaghfirullah..." she cried meekly. "I seek forgiveness from Allah!"

She had indeed lived a fine and blessed life, for she was none other than Aisha, as-Siddiqah, the truthful one, daughter of Abu Bakr as-Siddiq, and wife of the greatest man to walk the Earth. What's more, she could recall every detail of every incident she had lived through. It was as if each moment was vividly seared upon her heart.

After Ibn Abbas had left, Aisha wandered through the corridors of her memories. Her gaze grew distant as she remembered where it all began: in the home of a merchant named Abu Bakr, in the bustling city of Makkah, where a vivacious young girl once played...

CHAPTER 2
Best Friends

Uqbah in Abi Mu'ayt had just finished playing a game of dice with his friends and was now heading towards the Ka'bah to pay his respects to the idols. His cloak swept the ground behind him, and his blue silk turban, along with his delicate saffron robe, distinguished him as a nobleman of Makkah.

Though he was a giant of a man, the craggy peak of Mount Abu Qubais rose to dizzying heights way above him. He trudged down the winding path towards the Holy Sanctuary with the sun beating down on him. Today, the sky was a brilliant, cloudless blue, and the fresh scent of jasmine blossom invigorated his senses.

Uqbah greeted newly arrived merchants with a jovial wave as he walked past the grand marquee of Bayn ad-Darayn, where caravans unloaded their camels upon reaching Makkah. Merchant caravans were the lifeblood of the city and every notable household in Makkah had a stake in them. The Makkans took Arabian goods like frankincense, copper and pearls to sell up north in Shaam, in the cities of Bosra and Damascus. From there, they purchased Roman goods and brought them back to Makkah for the booming Hajj season. In winter, they would carry their wares onward to Yemen to sell them and purchase the finest silks, Indian weaponry, spices and jewellery to bring back to Makkah for the next trade season.

Abu Bakr was attending to his shop at the corner of Layl Market. As a wealthy cloth merchant, his shop boasted the finest fabrics in Makkah: Chinese silk, striped Yemeni textiles, Indian brocade, linens, and embroidered cotton dyed in rich colours. The rolls of fabric were meticulously arranged by material, inviting shoppers to admire and purchase them by the cubit. From the corner of his eye, Abu Bakr caught sight of the burly figure of Uqbah heading towards the Banu Shaybah Gate. This grand archway, marked by a large wooden beam and white columns, served as the entrance to the Ka'bah complex.

Uqbah strolled past the rocky hillocks of Safa and Marwa, continuing through the gate until he reached the well of Zamzam. The Ka'bah stood majestically before him, its four sides draped with fine colourful fabrics. The Zamzam well with its cobbled walls had two long basins next to it, made of hollowed-out stone. One was for washing and one for drinking. Someone had already drawn water into the basins using the leather bucket, which dangled from a rope tied to a wooden pulley across the mouth of the well. Uqbah headed for the drinking basin, dunked his hand into it, and scooped the sweet water into his mouth, wetting his face.

Makkah was a hidden treasure in Arabia's scorching wilderness, surrounded by mountains and valleys, in the land of nomadic Bedouin tribes, golden camels and emerald palm trees. Known as the Mother of all Cities - *Umm al-Qura* - it attracted thousands annually to the House of Allah.

But it was a far cry from the time of the Prophets Ibrahim and Ismail, who had built the Ka'bah for the worship of Allah alone. Now, hundreds of idols filled the Ka'bah and its surroundings, and the descendants of Ismail - the Arabs - had largely forgotten the original call of their great ancestor.

Uqbah splashed water on his face and continued strolling towards the Ka'bah. Along the way, he passed by the tented canopy of Maqam Ibrahim, where the great ancestor once stood to build the house for Allah. Suddenly his eye fell upon a figure with his forehead to the ground, right in front of the sacred house. He shook his head, dazed for a moment as he took in the spectacle of the prayerful and perfumed

Prophet Muhammad ﷺ, with his cascading black hair, sitting, then bowing, then standing with no idol before him. The Prophet's ﷺ resplendent face came into view with its perfectly proportioned lips and cheekbones, moving in serene recitation.

The Prophet Muhammad ﷺ had been preaching his message for many years now in Makkah, calling people away from the worship of created things and to the worship of the Creator alone. But the people of Makkah feared his message, thinking it would affect their trade and businesses as well. The idols were both their worship and their revenue, attracting wealthy visitors to Makkah who seemed ever willing to lighten their pockets with gold and silver coins in the Holy City. The Makkans admitted that the Prophet Muhammad ﷺ was the most honest man amongst them, which is why they called him *as-Sadiq al-Ameen*, the Truthful and Trustworthy. However, they feared the power of his message and chose to oppress his followers.

"*Mudhammam*! You troublemaker!" Uqbah exploded in a fit of rage, lunging towards the Prophet Muhammad ﷺ, who remained unperturbed, deep in prayer. *Mudhammam* was the horrible nickname Uqbah and his comrades had given the Prophet ﷺ. It meant 'The Humiliated One', which was the exact opposite of the meaning of his blessed name Muhammad - The Praised One.

"You dare to pray here at the Ka'bah?" Uqbah shrieked hysterically, tearing the cloak from his own back and twisting it around the Prophet's ﷺ neck like a makeshift noose. The Prophet Muhammad ﷺ squeezed his eyes closed in pain, gasping for breath, as he wrapped his fingers around the twisted fibres, trying desperately to remove the noose.

By then, dozens of onlookers had gathered. Some cheered for Uqbah, who continued to attack the blessed Prophet ﷺ with ugly glee. Some secret followers of the Prophet Muhammad ﷺ stood with downcast eyes in helpless shame. So great was their fear of becoming Uqbah's next victims that they dared not intervene. The colour drained from the Prophet Muhammad's ﷺ face as he struggled for air, unable to repel the sudden and vicious attack alone.

"He's choking... the sound is unbearable," muttered one of the onlookers, his voice trembling with horror as the brutal scene unfolded.

"Can't Uqbah do this somewhere else?" someone else commented, covering their eyes.

Time froze as the Ka'bah stood sombre and silent, bearing witness to the impending crime: a child of Ibrahim, a Prophet of Allah, being savagely strangled to death at its doorstep. Even the hundreds of idols surrounding the cubical structure appeared to grimace momentarily, while the mountains of Makkah shuddered at the torment of the Messenger of Allah ﷺ.

THWACK!

Out of nowhere, Uqbah felt the full force of another man shoving him to the ground. He grunted in pain. It was Abu Bakr, rushing to his friend's aid.

"Woe to you, enemy of Allah!" Abu Bakr scolded, his eyes ablaze with danger, his voice deathly fierce. The crowd turned on Abu Bakr, beating and kicking until his head was sticky with blood. Still, he fought them off, his protests booming through the Makkan valley. "Would you kill a man because he says, 'My Lord is Allah'?" he shouted at them.

Panting heavily, Abu Bakr squared up to Uqbah and locked eyes with him. "Would you slay a man who brings clear signs from your Lord?!"

The crowd backed off and began to disperse, with the last onlookers groaning and shuffling away in shame. Meanwhile, Abu Bakr, his hands red and his cheek streaked with dirt, continued to shield the Prophet Muhammad ﷺ. Tears hung in Abu Bakr's eyes and blood dripped from his head as he knelt down to hold his friend, Muhammad ﷺ, in his arms.

"Are you alright, Rasulullah?" Abu Bakr asked in a whisper, wrapping his cloak tenderly around the Prophet's ﷺ frame. "May my mother and father be ransomed for you!" Then he pulled his beloved friend's arm over his shoulder until it was locked comfortably in place and helped him up.

Umm Ruman had just settled her little daughter, Aisha, down for the night when she spied two figures in the distance, through the window. Recognising the thin frame of her husband, Abu Bakr, she gasped at the sight of him limping and then swallowed hard. Her soft, worried eyes peered through the window as she pressed her lips together, fighting back tears. Meanwhile, the bruised and battered Prophet Muhammad ﷺ leaned on the slender yet strong shoulder of his friend, slowly regaining his strength.

"Asma!" Umm Ruman called urgently. "Come at once!"

A tall teenage girl with immaculately combed hair and almond eyes was sitting inside, doing some needle-work. Startled by her stepmother's distressed voice, she rushed to the door. Asma let out a yelp upon seeing her father's bloodied head. The tranquillity of the early evening shattered as she and Umm Ruman clattered about the house, gathering cushions, water and bandages to tend to the injured men.

"Shhhhhh!" said Umm Ruman, reminding Asma not to wake up her little sister.

Little Aisha remained undisturbed in the adjacent room, completely unaware of the commotion or her father's return home. She was peacefully dreaming, sound asleep.

CHAPTER 3
From Friends to Family

The Banu Taym, Abu Bakr's clan, dwelt south of the Ka'bah, between the rocky mountains of Jabal Kayd and Jabal Aqir. From the walled courtyard of Abu Bakr's house, the sound of prayer rose. It was here that he had established the first little masjid. Fine camels grazed outside, well-fed in preparation for the impending summer journey to Shaam.

When he led prayers, Abu Bakr recited the Quran with such tearful emotion that the women and children from neighbouring households secretly crept out of their homes to join in. They yearned to hear the soul-stirring recitation of Abu Bakr, much to the chagrin of their menfolk.

Young Aisha hopped and skipped in and out of the house, with her rosy cheeks, smiling eyes and nimble step. She was a gorgeous child and the apple of her father's eye.

Old beggars wearing only waist-cloths, along with slaves and street urchins, could be seen entering the house. They left, joyful that their needs had been met, their pots refilled, and their stomachs satiated by the generosity of Aisha's father. Their prayerful home and open hearts began attracting more and more people to the worship of Allah. This annoyed the leaders of Makkah to no end since they had been doing what they could to extinguish the Prophet Muhammad's ﷺ message from their city.

"Prayer without gods in front of you?" they'd ridicule. "What kind of prayer is that?"

"Abu Bakr is corrupting the youth!" they moaned, plotting to stop him from praying in the little masjid he had established in his own courtyard. But try as they may, Aisha's father carried on praying publicly and continued helping the Messenger of Allah ﷺ to call people back to the worship of Allah alone, without any partners, and away from the worship of man-made idols.

Aisha would prance around barefoot, chatting with her friends and untroubled by the cares of life. The home was spacious enough, with multiple rooms for their various needs. There was a pantry to prepare food and a separate storage room for the rolls and reams of fabric from the shop. The living room was the nicest room, with patterned couches lining its walls, and comfortable cushions especially for guests. There was a decorative rug in the middle with a raised table upon which food could be served.

Aisha focused on her toys and games but would look up every so often and keenly scan the goings-on of the home. Her grandfather, Abu Quhafah, sat upon a cushioned chair in the living room, keeping an eye on her, with his head perched upon a walking stick. He was a blind old man with a great wispy white beard who muttered to himself, shaking his head disapprovingly.

In fact, Abu Quhafah was one of the tribal leaders of Banu Taym, whose ancestors went all the way back to Prophet Ismail through his descendant, Adnan. He scoffed at the idea of embracing the Prophet Muhammad's ﷺ message and scowled whenever Aisha's father mentioned it. This was despite the fact that he respected the Prophet ﷺ and they shared a common ancestor about six generations back.

"Still ransoming feeble slaves, O Abu Bakr?" Abu Quhafah asked disparagingly. The Makkan chiefs were torturing slaves who embraced Islam, and Abu Bakr had made it his business to buy and then release them from their cruel masters so they could worship Allah without fear.

"Why bother freeing the powerless, penniless ones, my son, when they cannot protect you from your clansmen? You should find some strong, powerful men who can actually defend you!"

Aisha watched as her father approached his own father, squatting down beside the elderly man with a gentle smile.

"Dearest father," he said, "I only do what I do to please Allah." He placed a loving kiss upon Abu Quhafah's wrinkled brow before darting out of the room with a flick of his cloak.

Aisha's full brother, Abdurrahman, was at least 10 years older than her. Despite his many good qualities, like their grandfather, he remained stubborn and had not yet embraced Islam. On the other hand, her half-siblings Asma and Abdullah wholeheartedly embraced the Prophet's ﷺ message. They captivated Aisha. Asma, with her dark eyes, flowing dresses and stylishly tied waist belts, seemed like a princess from a fairy tale to her. Abdullah, always by their father's side and ever reliable, assisted in the family's shop. Although they did not all share the same mother, they were an integral part of Aisha's world, and she looked to them with great admiration.

Khawla bint Hakim felt restless. Two long years had passed since Khadijah, the Prophet's ﷺ beloved wife, had left this worldly realm, leaving him overcome with grief. She was worried about the Prophet ﷺ and decided to visit him to put forward a suggestion.

"O Messenger of Allah, have you thought about getting married again?" she said, thinking that if the Prophet ﷺ found love and companionship again, it might ease his heartache.

"To whom?" the Prophet ﷺ replied.

"You can choose to marry a young lady who has never been married or someone mature who has been married before."

The Prophet ﷺ asked her if she had anyone in mind.

"Aisha, daughter of your closest Companion, is the unmarried one, and the mature lady is Sawdah bint Zam'ah, who is a true Believer."

The Prophet ﷺ considered the suggestions. Sawdah was a pious lady who was a widow. As for Aisha, the Prophet ﷺ was surprised at the prospect. He had coincidentally seen a recurring dream where an angel carried someone to him wrapped in a silken piece of cloth. In the dream, the angel instructed him, "Lift the cover, for she is your wife!" Much to his surprise, it was Aisha.

Now the Prophet's ﷺ dreams were divine guidance and so he had told himself, "If this is from Allah, then it will happen."

When Khawla made the suggestion, the Prophet ﷺ gave her permission to go and propose to both Aisha's family and Sawdah's.

One day, when Aisha's father had gone out for business, there came a knock at the door. Aisha's mother, Umm Ruman, went to answer it. It was Khawla bint Hakim, beaming from their front porch. "O Umm Ruman!" she said excitedly. "Look at what Allah has bestowed upon you of goodness and blessings!"

Umm Ruman smiled politely but looked somewhat puzzled, unsure of the exact nature of the news. "Please, come in," she said, opening the door wider to let Khawla enter, and waited for her to continue.

"The Messenger of Allah ﷺ has sent me," Khawla informed her, "with a proposal to ask for your daughter Aisha's hand in marriage."

Umm Ruman gasped, covering her smile in disbelief, her dark eyes shining with anticipation. What an honour! Aisha's betrothal to the noble and gallant Prophet ﷺ would be a great blessing for their family!

In Makkan society, it was normal for girls and boys to be engaged or married at a young age. This was a way to strengthen relationships between families and to make sure that young people had a secure future to look forward to. The marriage might take place when they were young, but the couple would live together as husband and wife at a later time when they had reached maturity.

Umm Ruman paused, blinking thoughtfully. "I just remembered," she said, wincing, "that Aisha is actually engaged to marry Jubayr, the son of Mut'im bin Adi."

Khawla raised her eyebrows in surprise, and her smile faded. She was lost for words.

"I had better speak to Abu Bakr about it when he comes home," Umm Ruman concluded, "for by Allah, Abu Bakr has never made a promise except that he has kept it."

Khawla nodded in agreement.

Makkah was home to at least eight major marketplaces, each specialising in different trades. In the sheep market, a cacophony of bleating filled the air, mingling with the lively chatter of merchants showing off their livestock to young shepherds. Nearby, the poultry market resounded with the clucking and crowing of chickens, turkeys and various birds. Customers could select their birds to be slaughtered and de-feathered on the spot, ready for dinner that very day. The blacksmiths' market clattered from dawn till dusk, thick with the scent of heated metal as swords were tempered, spearheads hammered, shields crafted and tools sharpened.

Hanatin Market buzzed as a food hub, where vendors piled high grains like barley, millet, and wheat alongside dried dates, raisins, figs and pungent spices, selling them by the handful.

As for Hazwarah Market, it was the largest in Makkah and seemed to offer anything one could desire. Poets and entertainers gathered here, sharing literary masterpieces and seeking patronage from wealthy chieftains and noblewomen, often leaving with silver or - if they were lucky - gold pieces.

Abu Bakr's shop was a small converted house situated on the corner of Layl Market, which housed the more exclusive shops. All around, smoke from oud burners twirled up into the

sky, carrying a romantic fragrance that wafted up customers' noses, enticing them to explore the stores.

An eerie silence enveloped Layl Market at dusk when the last tradesmen closed up shop, extinguishing their incense burners. Abu Bakr retrieved the rolls of unsold cloth, secured the shutters, and took a moment to breathe in the fresh air of Makkah before heading home.

Upon Abu Bakr's return, Umm Ruman joyfully shared the news of the Prophet's ﷺ proposal for Aisha. Abu Bakr's face lit up. He could hardly believe his ears! They understood that such a momentous proposal was a tremendous blessing for their beloved Aisha and their entire family.

It's only right, Abu Bakr thought, stroking his beard, *that I discuss the matter with Mut'im first*.

Although Mut'im bin Adi was not a Muslim, he had played a crucial role in supporting Banu Hashim - the Prophet's ﷺ family - during the harsh years of the boycott imposed by the Quraysh. Mut'im had aided the Muslims when they were expelled from their homes and forced to endure living in tents without access to food. Abu Bakr was unsure how Mut'im now felt about his son, Jubayr, marrying Aisha, but since he was a man of his word, he would discuss it with him, respecting their old agreement.

So the next day, Abu Bakr visited Mut'im at his home in the Banu Nawfal district near the Ka'bah. As Abu Bakr spoke, Mut'im's brow furrowed and fear flashed across his face. His wife sat upright, lips pursed, shifting in her seat.

"We are afraid," she said, her expression hardening as she spoke, "that if we marry Jubayr to Aisha, you will persuade him to abandon the religion of our forefathers." And so, they informed Aisha's father in no uncertain terms that they no longer wanted their son to marry her.

Umm Ruman heaved a sigh of relief and Abu Bakr was beaming as they sent a message to the Messenger of Allah ﷺ inviting him to solemnise the marriage contract in the customary manner.

Since Aisha was still young, she would continue living with her parents and siblings, enjoying her usual activities until the time was right. The only change Aisha noticed was that her mother began treating her as though she were exceptionally special. Suddenly, she became concerned about Aisha's well-being and began offering her special foods to eat. She also started calling her by a new nickname - *Areesa* - which meant 'little bride'.

Sawdah bint Zam'ah had also accepted the Prophet's ﷺ proposal. And so it was that Aisha and Sawdah were married to the Prophet Muhammad ﷺ and only Allah could know what the future had in store for them.

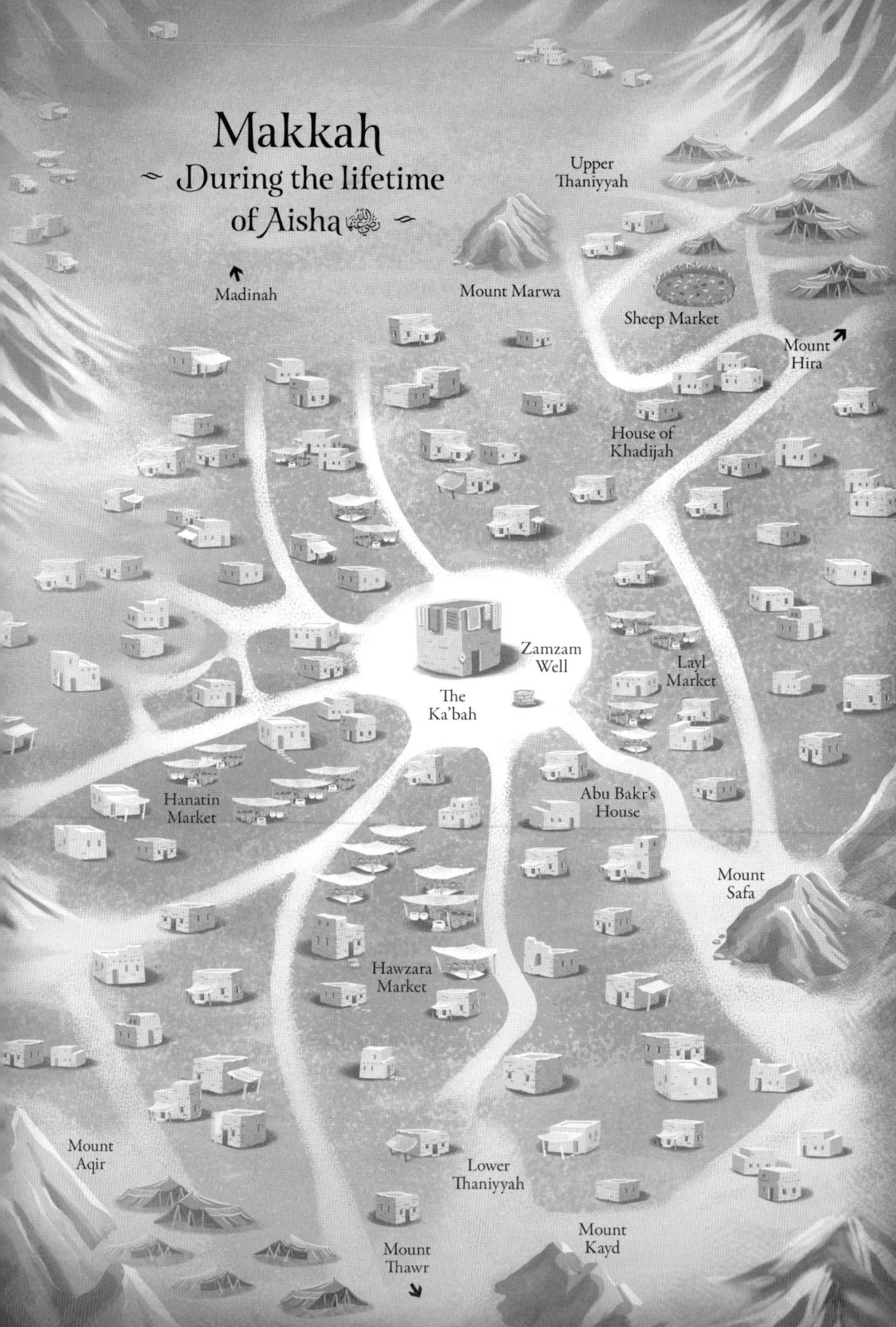

Makkah
During the lifetime
of Aisha
Madinah
Upper
Thaniyyah
Mount Marwa
Sheep Market
Mount
Hira
House of
Khadijah
Zamzam
Well
The
Ka'bah
Layl
Market
Hanatin
Market
Abu Bakr's
House
Mount
Safa
Hawzara
Market
Mount
Aqir
Lower
Thaniyyah
Mount
Kayd
Mount
Thawr

CHAPTER 4
The Calm Before the Storm

Darkness had fallen over Makkah and the loud din of people and animals jostling through the streets increased as they hurried home before the light slipped away. When night fell, the only light they had was the dim glow of terracotta oil lamps and candles. Sometimes the glorious full moon would shine down so brightly upon the streets of Makkah that it seemed to cast a shadow, and daily business could carry on a little longer.

Two fat camels stood in the courtyard of Abu Bakr's house. They had drunk so much that all the water had run out and Umm Ruman had to fetch more water from the local well. They were being fed the leaves of the Samurra tree in anticipation of an impending journey.

Aisha rubbed her eyes and yawned. She'd spent the entire day frolicking with friends on the swing near their home, and her toys - which were simple rag dolls made of linen and straw, and carved wooden animals - were strewn all over the floor. Her personal favourite was a wooden winged horse. What a fantastical beast it was! How wonderful it would be to ride such a horse!

Aisha was by now feeling rather dusty and sleepy. She decided to rearrange her toys one last time, just to make sure they were all there, before retiring to bed. In the adjacent room, her father sat, speaking in tight, hushed tones. The gentle flicker of an oil lamp was all that lit up Abu Bakr's face, revealing the fine creases on his forehead. Next to him sat the Messenger of Allah ﷺ, a reassuring hand gently placed upon his friend's arm.

"Please give me permission to leave Makkah, O Messenger of Allah," pleaded Abu Bakr. His red, henna-tinged beard glistened every time the candlelight fluttered.

The Muslims in Makkah had faced a lot of hardship because of the powerful leaders of the Quraysh tribe. Many of the poorest Muslims were tortured, and even the Prophet's ﷺ family and friends were forced out of their homes. Eventually, they were allowed to return, but they knew the Quraysh were still plotting against them. Some Muslims had already crossed the Red Sea into Abyssinia, where a kindly Christian king had accepted them.

At one point, the persecution had gotten too much, so Abu Bakr had also tried to leave for Abyssinia. But when Ibn ad-Daghnah, the chief of the Qara tribe, had seen him travelling outside Makkah with all of his belongings in tow, he fiercely objected.

"Where on earth are you going?" Ibn ad-Daghnah had asked, his hands on his hips.

"My people have driven me from my land," Abu Bakr explained, "and I, for one, wish to live freely in this world and worship my Lord."

Ibn ad-Daghnah couldn't believe his ears. "A man like you should not be turned out of his land!" he exclaimed. "You help the poor earn their living, keep good relations with your relatives, help those in need, provide guests with food and shelter, and help those who are in trouble. What are the Quraysh thinking?" He was so perturbed that he marched Abu Bakr back to Makkah and pleaded with the leaders of the Quraysh to place Abu Bakr under his protection.

The leaders of Makkah allowed Abu Bakr to return on the condition that he wouldn't pray in public. However, he established the masjid in his courtyard, which soon drew the attention of everyone who passed by. The Quraysh summoned Ibn ad-Daghnah, who went to Abu Bakr, telling him they would revoke his protected status if Abu Bakr didn't stop praying openly. Abu Bakr thanked Ibn ad-Daghnah for his concern but told him, "I repeal your pledge of protection and am content with Allah as my protector!"

But now, more Muslims searching for a safe haven were leaving Makkah. During the Hajj season, members of the Aws and Khazraj tribes from the troubled city of Yathrib had met the wise Prophet ﷺ and accepted Islam. They were now inviting him to help resolve their feuds, offering him protection and a new home.

The moment felt just right. At long last, they would find safety there and could worship Allah in peace. Yathrib's promise to stand by the Prophet ﷺ and protect the Believers was what they had been looking for. The Prophet ﷺ gave many people permission to leave for the welcoming new city - a land of date palm trees, nestled between two mountains and two rocky tracts, as the Prophet ﷺ had described to them from a dream he had seen.

The candle flame danced in the Prophet's ﷺ eyes, and his cheeks glowed. His prominent, arched eyebrows rose as he searched his friend's worried face. "Do not rush," he said, "for perhaps Allah will provide you with a companion for your journey. I expect to be permitted to emigrate soon."

At this, Abu Bakr became animated. "May my father be sacrificed for your sake! Are you truly expecting that?" he asked. The Prophet ﷺ replied in the affirmative.

Ever since Aisha could remember, the Prophet Muhammad ﷺ had visited her father almost every day. They always seemed to talk about such serious matters and then they would pray together. Now, from the corner of her eye, just as her dolls were about to retreat to their beds, she saw the faint forms of the two men projected against the wall. Their shadows stood shoulder to shoulder, bowed down and then returned to full height, one after the other, before disappearing onto the ground in prostration.

Trouble had long been brewing in Makkah and they had heard that the Quraysh were now plotting to assassinate the Prophet ﷺ. Something had to be done before it was too late. Abu Bakr took a deep breath and settled back into his seat. They knew they had to wait for Allah's permission, trusting that His plan was always the best one.

Aisha sat singing little songs and happily putting her things away, ready for their adventures the next day. Her father seemed on edge. She sensed something was wrong but could not yet grasp the gravity of the events unfolding around her. These events would shape not only the future of Makkah but the entire world, making her an important part of Allah's plan.

Aisha crept into her bed. She felt safe, wrapped up in her warm, woolly blanket. She closed her eyes, sure that the two wise men in the next room would take care of her no matter what was happening. The honeyed voice of Rasulullah ﷺ, reciting the Quran while leading her father in prayer ebbed and flowed in her head as she drifted away and the world was engulfed in silence.

CHAPTER 5
The Storm

Aisha stood on a footstool with poise and recited the entire lineage of Banu Taym from memory. Abu Bakr's eyes lit up. "Well done!" he cheered, impressed by her precision. He was an expert in the genealogy of the Arabs, and it looked like his daughter was about to follow in his footsteps. Knowledge of the ancestors was more than just memorising names. It was an education in the history of their heritage, land, tribal kinship, warriors and romances.

"Again, dear Father!" Aisha said, beaming eagerly as her father, sitting in his favourite chair in the living room, shared new lines of poetry. She would stare intently, her round black eyes sparkling with concentration, and would memorise every word. Aisha's voice was clear and confident. Today she practised reciting verses from the poet Abu Kabeer al-Hudhali in praise of his beloved son:

"To gaze upon his handsome face in all its majesty,
Is to glimpse the moon, lighting the world for all to see."

Asma clapped, glowing with approval at the eloquent recital. Then came the poetry of Labeed, which Aisha had learned by heart:

"Everything except for Allah will perish,
And all happiness, unconditionally, shall vanish,
Journeying through the night, man thinks he has achieved.
Yet a lifetime he spends yearning, then bereaved."

Asma clapped again to encourage her sister. But then let out a sigh and began rubbing her own back. She had recently married the great Companion of the Prophet ﷺ, az-Zubayr bin al-Awwam, and her abdomen blossomed with the growth of her first child. Aisha was looking forward to having a new baby in the family.

As noon approached, the sun became an unbearable furnace, and all work ceased. People retired for the shade and for a *qaylulah*, their midday nap. Just then, a gentle yet distinctive 'rat-a-tat-tat' sounded at the door – a familiar knock, but at an unexpected hour. They scanned each other's faces. "What could the matter be at this time?" they wondered.

A servant boy shuffled in and whispered, "It is the Messenger of Allah ﷺ but he has his face covered up!"

Abu Bakr leapt to his feet at once. "May my father and mother be sacrificed for him!" he said emphatically. "By Allah, he has not come at this time, except for something urgent."

The turbaned Prophet ﷺ peered at them over his face-covering, the whites of his eyes flickering. He pulled down the cloth that was wrapped around his face, revealing his lush black beard and locked eyes with Abu Bakr. He was about to speak but then paused.

"Tell everyone who is here to leave," the Prophet ﷺ whispered cautiously. Whatever he had come for was top secret and had to be kept from the wrong ears.

Abu Bakr pointed towards his daughters, Aisha and Asma, and reassured him. "There is no one here but your family, O Messenger of Allah," he said. "May my father be sacrificed for you!"

The Prophet ﷺ nodded and his shoulders relaxed. Once again, he looked Abu Bakr straight in the eye and spoke with deliberation.

"I have been given permission..." he said, "...to migrate."

Abu Bakr almost jumped with delight. "Will I be accompanying you, O Messenger of Allah?" he asked, pausing with bated breath.

"Yes," replied the Prophet ﷺ, smiling. He knew that being by his side on the journey to Yathrib meant the world to Abu Bakr.

Abu Bakr's eyes welled up and he looked heavenward. Aisha glanced at Asma, searching for an explanation. She had never seen anyone cry tears of joy before. In fact, she hadn't known it was even possible.

Then Abu Bakr's demeanour changed. He began pacing up and down the room, thinking through his action plan. "O Messenger of Allah," he said, "I have prepared two she-camels especially for this journey. You must take one of them," he insisted. Abu Bakr had been feeding and watering his she-camels well and was confident that they could go for days in the desert without water.

The Arabian camel or dromedary was the ultimate desert transport. The four-legged animal could walk for miles and travel for days without refuelling. This made it worth a great deal of money. The Prophet ﷺ nodded, saying, "I will accept it on the condition that you let me pay for it." Abu Bakr waved away any notion of this with the back of his hand.

Asma rose to her feet, smoothed down her dress, and adjusted her belt. By now, Umm Ruman was wide awake and had heard the news. They muttered something to each other and set to work.

Umm Ruman's heart pounded, but she kept her emotions hidden. Still, Aisha caught the glint of tears gathering in her mother's eyes. With a furrowed brow and tight voice, Umm

Ruman instructed Asma and Aisha, and the girls quickly set to work, packing what was needed for the arduous journey ahead: water skins, black Ajwah dates, dried meat and a couple of daggers for protection.

Abu Bakr and the Prophet ﷺ had to leave immediately. There was no time to lose. They were about to make the most dangerous journey of their lives and every man with a sword in Makkah would be hot on their heels.

Asma placed the food into a brown leather bag and filled the water skins, lugging them outside to hoist them onto their saddles. Aisha saw her put the items on the ground and look around frantically for something to tie the bags with.

"My father," Asma gasped, "I have nothing to tie the containers with, except..." She looked down at her beautiful long dress. She was wearing her favourite matching waist belt.

Abu Bakr scratched his beard. "Divide it lengthwise, in two," he suggested. Aisha looked on, wondering what Asma would do. Pretty Asma always took care of her precious clothes. To Aisha's surprise, Asma untied the belt and began pulling it off her waist. Then she bit a small tear into it and ripped it right down the middle, splitting it in two. She used one half to fasten the food and tied the other half back around her waist.

When the Prophet ﷺ saw this, he smiled and said, "*Dhat an-Nitaqain*! The Lady with the Two Belts," bestowing upon her this special title. Asma's readiness to sacrifice something dear to her for the sake of Allah visibly moved him. She had torn her belt in two just to assist them. The Prophet ﷺ told her she would receive two special belts in Paradise in return for her act.

Asma beamed upon hearing this and her dark, kohl-filled eyes lit up. She pressed her lips together gleefully, for she knew that the Prophet's ﷺ glad tidings always came true. This meant that she was destined for Paradise.

Paradise!

The magnificent home in the hereafter for Allah's faithful servants.

Paradise!

With its flowing rivers of milk and honey, its palaces and finery, its fruits that tasted more delicious than anything this world had to offer and anything she could imagine. Indeed, the gowns and belts of Paradise would be more ornate than the regalia and jewellery worn by the wealthiest royalty on Earth.

Umm Ruman's tender face looked red, her apron damp with tears. Abu Bakr held his family members in a warm embrace and made *du'a* for them. He bent down and kissed Aisha on her pink cheek. As soon as his Bedouin guide arrived, the two companions waved farewell and climbed onto their mounts.

The guide was Ibn Urayqeet, a true man of the desert with his leathery tanned skin, strong aquiline nose and deep-set eyes.

"Fi amanillah," Abu Bakr whispered, "I entrust you all to Allah."

Aisha watched their camels from the window, zig-zagging through the valley and disappearing into the blazing sun. "I'll send for you soon!" Aisha thought she heard her father say, as a warm breeze drifted in with a whiff of the desert, and the lingering threat of capture.

A vicious band of young men, muscles bulging and armed to the hilt with spears and swords, had gathered outside the Prophet's ﷺ house to the north of Makkah. Each of them hailed from a different clan and each had only one mission: to kill the Prophet Muhammad ﷺ when he came out at dawn. Lurking in the shadows, they had masked their faces to hide their identities. The leader amongst them, a tall man with a menacing frown, skulked up to the window of the Prophet's ﷺ house and pointed towards it.

"Muhammad is sleeping in there," he whispered to his comrades, locking eyes with them. "We will wait here till he comes out at dawn. Let's make sure it's his final night!"

Then, although he had been the noisiest of them all, the leader lifted a finger to his mouth and hissed, "Shhhhhhh!"

At the first crack of dawn, someone unbolted the door. The bloodthirsty bunch held their spears and swords aloft, preparing to strike. *At last,* they thought, *we will cure the disease that is afflicting Makkah and put an end to Muhammad and his message!*

As they pulled back their weapons, ready to strike, the door creaked open. All of a sudden, their leader, with a menacing frown, bellowed, "Stop!"

As he yelled out, a muscular arm shot forward to restrain the lunging assassins. "Don't strike! It is Ali!" he screeched.

Ali was the Prophet's ﷺ young cousin, son of his beloved uncle Abu Talib. He had agreed to sleep in his bed that night to throw the Quraysh off the trail.

The grim men were startled. They took one look at Ali and fled, bewildered at the Prophet's ﷺ sudden disappearance and fearful that Banu Hashim would find out about their wicked plan and seek revenge. Banu Hashim were, after all, Ali and the Prophet's ﷺ clan.

Two major valleys served as exits from Makkah: the Upper Pass to the north; and to the south, near Abu Bakr's house, the Lower Pass. The usual route to Yathrib was from the north. But Abu Bakr and the Prophet ﷺ had departed from the south, between Jabal Kayd and Jabal Aqir, where the Quraysh leaders would least expect them.

Now, sunrise was upon them and soon the bounty hunters would arrive, riding upon their camels, clutching daggers and scouring the sand dunes for signs of the two fugitives.

"O people! 100 camels for the one who finds Muhammad and his companion!" was the cry that rang throughout the city. No stone was to be left unturned.

They deployed trackers to search all around Makkah. They were expert Bedouins who could trace desert travellers with the smallest of clues. Legend had it they could tell which bird had flown through an area just by smelling the air.

Back in Makkah, Aisha didn't know when she'd see her father and the Messenger of Allah ﷺ again, but she hoped it would be soon.

CHAPTER 6
Asma

"*Yaa Asma*! Where are you?" Abu Quhafah croaked.

"Coming *Yaa Jaddi*!" Asma replied, appearing before him.

"Has your father left?" asked Abu Quhafah.

"Yes, dear grandfather, he has."

"Without leaving a penny," he continued. "Huh! What has Abu Bakr left you with? Adversity? Poverty? Penury? He has deprived you of himself and his wealth!"

"No, no, Grandfather! Father has left us with plenty," said Asma. She held out a bulging cloth pouch, gently guiding her grandfather's hand to feel its weight.

The blind old man felt the pouch with his hand and leaned back in his chair, satisfied that Abu Bakr had left a good number of gold coins for his family. "Well, if that is what he has left you with, then there is no blame upon him," he concluded.

Asma's and Aisha's eyes met. They were both well aware there was nothing but pebbles in that pouch. Asma didn't want her grandfather to fall ill with worry and so she eased his heart without uttering a single untruth. The Hijrah to Yathrib was such a dangerous journey that Abu Bakr had taken every bit of his 6,000 dirhams with him to help the Messenger of Allah ﷺ. Asma's husband, az-Zubayr, was away on a long trade journey to Shaam, leaving them with scant resources to live on. She knew their father hadn't left them with much that could be counted, but had left them with Allah to *count on*. He trusted that during this critical time, what they had at home would suffice them, and Allah would take care of them until he had reached safety and sent for them.

BANG! BANG! THUD!

Aisha's heart nearly stopped at the terrifying pounding coming from the door. Asma held her back and stood up, her eyes darting left and right, thinking what to do.

BANG! THUD! BANG!

And now a gruff voice was yelling, too. "Open up! Open the door!"

The front door was bulging inward and shaking so violently it looked ready to fall off its hinges. Asma took a deep breath and then exhaled. "Stay back," she instructed Aisha, before calmly heading for the door.

"One moment! Please wait!" Asma called out. "Who is it?"

"It is Abul Hakam! Open up *im-med-iately*!"

Abul Hakam, which meant 'Father of Wisdom', was a name that didn't suit him at all, given how he rejected the truth and treated the Muslims so cruelly. That's why everyone

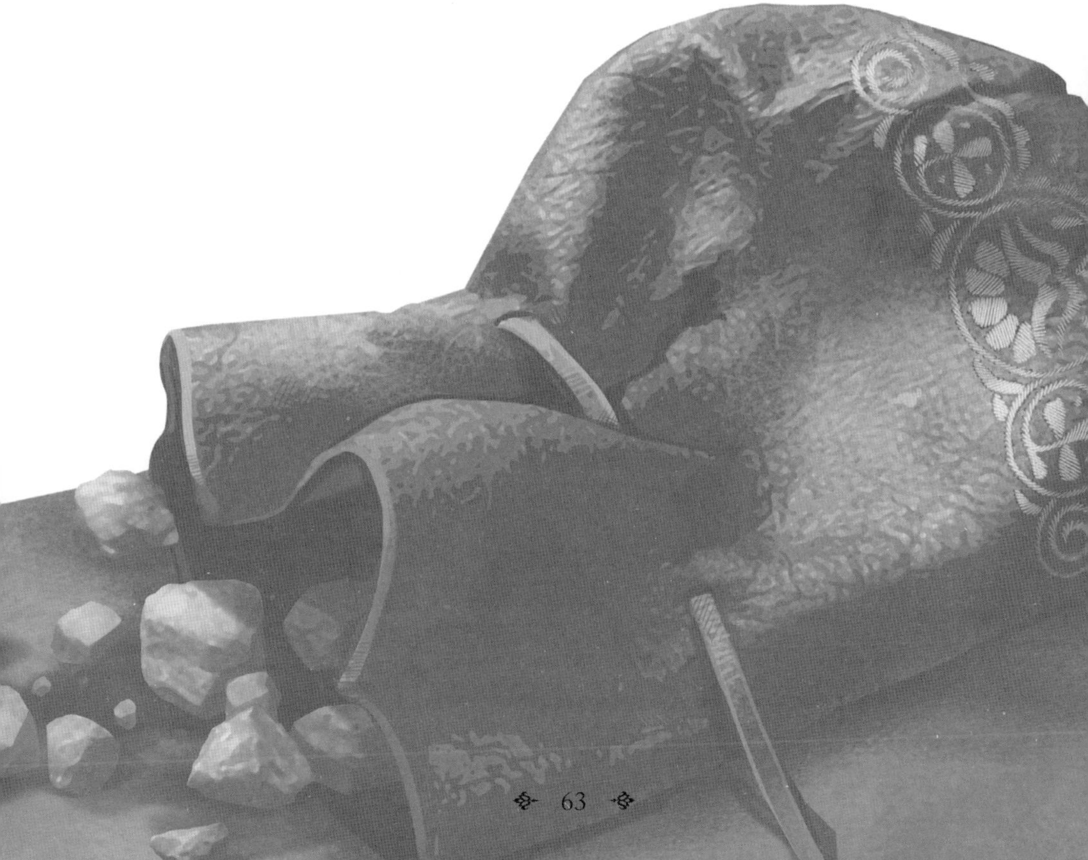

actually called him 'Abu Jahl' - 'Father of Ignorance' - a far more befitting name! He continued banging on the door, his voice full of rage.

Asma released the latch and opened the door to the fuming, beady-eyed, pot-bellied Abu Jahl.

"Where... is... your... father?" Abu Jahl hissed, pronouncing each word through gritted teeth and emphasising every syllable, as though she were a foreigner - or just plain stupid. Sweat drenched his scarlet face and a vein popped out in his neck as he yelled. He had a leather whip in his hand and there were dark circles around his eyes, betraying his lack of sleep.

Asma blinked nervously, her long eyelashes flickering as she searched for a response. Her legs ached as she was heavily pregnant and due to give birth any day now. Aisha peered from inside the house, wondering what would happen next as her sister looked Abu Jahl squarely in his squinting eyes.

"I don't know," Asma replied.

"Don't know? Don't know?" Abu Jahl's nostrils flared. "Do you take me for a fool?"

Suddenly the cruel chieftain lashed out in anger, slapping Asma across her face. The blow ripped her earring from her ear, streaking her throbbing cheek with blood. Her lower lip trembled, but she fought back tears and wiped the blood away. Aisha, huddled in the corner at the back of the room, cried out for her sister. Abu Jahl grunted with satisfaction and spat on the floor, feeling not a shred of shame. He turned to his stunned henchmen and stormed off past them.

Asma stood by the open door and closed her eyes, saying absolutely nothing. A fresh breeze enveloped her, and her dress fluttered in a moment of calm. Aisha, still in the corner, swallowed her fear and hurried to see if her brave sister was alright.

The young ladies squeezed each other in a long embrace, letting the tears flow. They remembered what their father had taught them: Allah was watching. Nothing escaped Allah and he would bring every criminal to justice one day. Every moment of pain would be rewarded. They just had to carry on obeying Allah and staying away from what Allah had forbidden. They had to be steadfast, to keep going - that's what *sabr* was.

Asma had a new title, given to her by the Messenger of Allah ﷺ: *Dhat an-Nitaqain*, the Lady With the Two Belts in Paradise. What a fitting title! What an honour! Everything Aisha had witnessed that day only confirmed to her that Asma was truly more than a princess. Asma was a woman of Jannah.

CHAPTER 7
Newborn Hope

For three long months, Aisha sat at the window, longing for her father. Thankfully, they had heard that Abu Bakr and the Prophet ﷺ arrived in the town of Yathrib safely and renamed it al-Madinah al-Munawwarah - The Enlightened City. But their families were still in Makkah, still in danger.

Every night, Umm Ruman would gather Aisha and her siblings and try to raise their spirits. She'd raise her hands to Allah and pray for good news.

The Makkan chiefs began seizing the property of Muslims who had fled to Madinah. They took over their shops, stole their belongings and grabbed their prized possessions. Life was becoming more dangerous by the day for the

Believers. The Quraysh kept a watchful eye on Abu Bakr's house and shop, waiting for their chance to pounce. It was only a matter of time before they would close in on their home.

Then, one day, all of a sudden and out of the blue, Aisha's half-brother, Abdullah, came home panting and gesticulating.

"Zayd and Abu Rafi are here," he exclaimed, his large round eyes even larger and more animated than usual. Zayd was the Prophet's ﷺ adopted son. He was a former Arab slave who had been gifted to the Prophet ﷺ by Khadijah. As for Abu Rafi, he was an Egyptian slave gifted to the Prophet ﷺ by his uncle, al-Abbas. He had embraced Islam and was a trusty assistant to the Prophet ﷺ.

Abdullah was so excited that he was huffing and puffing between words. "Father... Father has sent Ibn Urayqeet, his desert guide, with a letter instructing us to join them."

The Prophet ﷺ had also sent supplies for his family, ensuring they could safely escape Makkah alongside Abu Bakr's household.

Umm Ruman grinned girlishly. "We must leave for Madinah immediately!" she declared. "At last, we will be reunited as a family." The girls cheered with joy.

There was a great bustle in the house and much running around and packing of luggage. The Messenger of Allah ﷺ had sent 500 dirhams and two camels to aid them on their journey. The Prophet's ﷺ household consisted of: his daughters, Fatima and Umm Kulthum; his other wife,

Sawdah; and his foster mother, Umm Ayman, with her son, Usama. Before long, they had laden their camels with whatever belongings they could manage, and the party departed. Out of nowhere, Aisha's brother, Abdurrahman, appeared.

"Do come with us, O Abdurrahman!" Umm Ruman pleaded with her son.

"I shall not!" Abdurrahman replied firmly. Umm Ruman held her gaze for what felt like a lifetime, looking up at the young man who now stood taller than her. Without another word, Abdurrahman turned and ran off to his friend's house. The light of Islam had not yet entered his heart and Umm Ruman knew all she could do now was pray for him.

"*Yalla,* Areesa!" called Umm Ruman. "It is time to leave!" With Zayd and Abu Rafi flanking them, they were going to be in safe hands.

"First you must lean back," one of the camel drivers told Aisha. "Then lean forward as the front of the camel comes up." By the time Aisha was on the crouching beast, she'd forgotten the instructions completely and only just managed not to fall off the saddle. She lurched forward as the animal stood up, first upon its hind legs, and then lurched back as it extended its front legs.

Ibn Urayqeet led the way. His leathery face was covered completely except for a slit for his eyes. This was more to protect from sandstorms and the arid desert wind than anything else. Zayd accompanied the Prophet's ﷺ household, which included Umm Ayman and Usama, as well as his own wife and son.

Asma bit her lip. She was now heavily pregnant and the thought of the long, hot journey filled her with dread. To make matters worse, an old soothsayer was spreading rumours throughout Makkah that the Muslims were cursed and that no child would be born to them alive. "Superstitious nonsense!" her elders had called it, dismissively. Nonetheless, no child had indeed been born alive to any Muslim family ever since the first of them left Makkah, and some worried that perhaps the curse was real.

Along the way, a dark-skinned man with long wavy hair came galloping towards them. He was none other than the great Companion, Talha bin Ubaydillah. He saluted them, honoured to make the Hijrah with them.

Aisha bobbed up and down on her camel, but managed to turn her head and catch a final glimpse of the city she called home, wondering if they would ever return. The sun disappeared behind the mountains of Makkah, and they became mere silhouettes against the starry night sky. Eventually, the mountains disappeared and the desert dunes took their place, surrounding them on all sides.

They rode, rode, rode - a dozen men, women and children on a dozen dromedaries - into the cold, deep, dark night. The next day, the sun blazed over their heads and everything shimmered and glimmered with blinding light.

Aisha could see nothing but dune after dune; reddish and orange dunes, golden-yellow dunes, dunes stretching endlessly behind one another. The swinging gait of her camel lulled her into a drowsy haze, making her forget both the home she had left behind and the long journey still ahead. Rocking back and forth, her senses grew heavy and she drifted into sleep. When she awoke, she noticed the wisps of golden grass growing sparsely on the crests of the dunes, with a few gnarled bushes twisting over the sand like mighty serpents.

Aisha's camel seemed to have its own ideas about the route it was taking. She tried her best to hold on to its reins as it darted right and left, unpredictably. Then, without warning, her camel began charging ahead so fast that Umm Ruman shrieked, fearing it would gallop with her daughter into the sandy abyss!

Umm Ruman was terrified. "O Areesa!" she screamed in alarm. "Watch out! Where are you going with my daughter?" Aisha held on for dear life as her camel zig-zagged away from the rest of the caravan. Was it trying to kidnap her? "Let go of the reins, Areesa!" Umm Ruman called out. "You are holding them too tight!"

Aisha's body lurched up and down on the camel's back as she let go of the reins and clasped the horn of the saddle. The camel was having none of it. It shot off, leaving a cloud of sand behind it, much to Umm Ruman's alarm.

When they eventually caught up with the camel, they heaved a sigh of relief as they realised its reins had become caught in the branch of a twisted tree and it was well and truly stuck. The reins must have flown through the air and hooked onto the blessed bush. The camel pulled and pulled, but it was no use. It had to give up. The other members of the caravan surrounded Aisha and ensured that, from now on, her camel would be doubly flanked by them to keep it in check.

As they approached the small town of Quba where the Prophet ﷺ had stopped during his journey and laid the foundation for the first masjid, Asma began feeling some twinges. It seemed the time had come for her baby to arrive. So the caravan stopped at Quba and Asma retreated to her tent.

"*Allahu Akbar!*" the Muslims cheered. The baby's cry, coming from Asma's tent, was like the sweetest melody they had ever heard.

"*Allahu Akbar!*" Once again, the cheers rang out.

Asma had given birth to a healthy baby boy. So jubilant were the Muslims that they lifted the new baby, Abdullah bin az-Zubayr, up high and passed him around the encampment.

When the news of Abdullah bin az-Zubayr's birth reached Madinah, the streets erupted with more cheers. "*Allahu Akbar!*" The cheers echoed across Madinah. The rumours of a curse had been false all along. Allah had given them a clear sign that life and death were in His hands alone.

Aisha's heart brimmed with love for her new nephew. She kissed Abdullah on his cheek tenderly, and as she gazed into his twinkling eyes, she knew they would never part.

CHAPTER 8
The Would-be King of Yathrib

Ibn Salul sank his teeth into his thumb and swore. "Curse and confound it!" he exclaimed, gritting his teeth with fury. His cavernous home loomed around him, a shadowy reflection of his own despair. With a forceful blow, he pounded his fist against a panel in the wall, the thud echoing through the empty halls.

"He's taking over my city!" Ibn Salul cried, his heart heavy with bitterness. "Yathrib belongs to me! I am the one who built it and now he seeks to steal it from me!"

Ibn Salul lived in a mansion in a pleasant suburb of Madinah, nestled among lush palm trees. It shared no wall with any other home and lorded over the rest, taller, colder, and less approachable than them all. It was as if it stood with its nose in the air, looking down disdainfully upon the dwellings around it.

Today, Ibn Salul was pacing around his room, his face contorted and twisted with indignation about what was happening to his beloved city Yathrib, now renamed Madinah.

"Did he think we would hand it over to him on a plate? Not likely!" he snarled. But the bitter truth was undeniable: they had handed Yathrib over. The Aws tribe and his own tribe, the Khazraj, had made peace through the Prophet's ﷺ efforts, uniting under his leadership and welcoming him with open arms. Ibn Salul's eyes drooped and he let out a heavy sigh as the full weight of it settled over him.

"What fools they are!" Ibn Salul muttered. "They didn't even consult me! How could they let him do this to me? How dare they rob me of my kingdom?"

Oh, but he was green with envy, was Ibn Salul! A scowling, snarling, crooked, beady-eyed, though strangely elegant, old scoundrel. He owed that elegance to his tailor, who created impeccably fitted garments for him, made of brocade and silks, fit for a king, so to speak.

For years, the two tribes in Yathrib, the Aws and the Khazraj, had been at each other's throats. They had been feuding and battling with no end in sight. Whenever there was a conflict, the Jews of the city would threaten them, saying, "When the promised Prophet comes, we will take over this city!" They said he was a Messenger from Allah. Their scriptures foretold it and they were awaiting his impending arrival.

Members of the two tribes had met the Prophet Muhammad ﷺ twice during the Hajj season, on the outskirts of Makkah, in the mountain pass of Aqabah, and learned about his message. They at once knew it was the truth and that this was the prophet foretold in the Jewish scriptures. No less than 75 of them had embraced Islam and pledged to protect the Prophet ﷺ. In return, they hoped he would help bring peace to their city and guide them all to Paradise.

Stepping out into his courtyard, Ibn Salul looked up at the sky. The blazing sun shone on his face with a blinding light. But he was too entangled in his own resentment and self-pity to care.

"I am the chief of Khazraj, the rightful king of this city! Yes, I am!" howled Ibn Salul, shaking a fist at the sky. "I would have brokered peace for Yathrib. None of them could have done it, save me!"

For as long as he could recall, the burning desire to hold sway over the land of Yathrib had flourished within him. It was an ambition that had consumed his every thought and shaped his every action. A ruler he would be, or die in the pursuit. Ibn Salul had bribed people, played politics and schemed his way to the top of society, only to see his dreams turn to dust before his eyes. Now, as he sat there feeling downcast, he absent-mindedly twirled the emerald ring on his finger and stared at the gold medallion hanging from his neck. These shiny trinkets brought him a little bit of comfort.

"All hope is not lost," he thought. "Sooner or later, the imbeciles will realise the folly of their decision. And at that point, I shall step in and reclaim my kingdom. In the meantime, I must play 'the long game'."

And so, Ibn Salul adjusted his cloak, straightened his turban, puffed out his chest and plastered a blood-chilling smile upon his face, before joining the merriment of the Muslims in their new masjid.

It was Friday, and the Muhajirun and Ansar had gathered in the new masjid that the Prophet ﷺ had helped to build. '*Muhajirun*' was the title given to the migrants from Makkah, and '*Ansar*' - or Helpers - was the title given to the residents of Madinah, who had welcomed them with open arms. The Muhajirun were refugees who had left their homes for the sake of Allah and travelled all the way to Madinah to be with the Prophet ﷺ. The Ansar had helped and supported the Prophet ﷺ and his Companions from Makkah. Now that they were brothers in faith, the Prophet ﷺ had honoured them with these new titles. Together, the Muhajirun and the Ansar were of the *Sahaba* - that special generation who saw, met, lived with and were disciples of, the blessed Prophet ﷺ.

The new masjid was a sight to behold. It was a square building made of mud bricks, around 35 metres long and

30 metres wide. Date palm leaves, cemented together with beaten clay and supported by palm trunks as pillars, formed the roof. Little glints of sunlight peeped through the gaps in the roof, and when it rained the masjid would get soaked. On the opposite side was the shelter for the homeless, a group called the *Ahl as-Suffah*.

If you sat anywhere else in the masjid and looked up, you'd see the stunning blue sky, and at night you could lay there counting the stars.

Next to the masjid, the Prophet ﷺ had ordered the construction of two houses. They were more like huts than houses, for each one was a simple square room made of mud bricks, with a small courtyard, a *hujrah*, surrounded by a fence. One was for his wife, Sawdah, and the other for Aisha, to be used once she was ready to reside in her matrimonial home.

Ibn Salul swanned into the masjid flamboyantly, turning heads as he went. No one knew what to expect from him, so they waited with bated breath to hear what he would say. Whispers circulated that he had disrespected the Prophet ﷺ in public, putting on a false display of disgust as if a foul stench permeated the air as he passed him by. His raucous protests against the new call to prayer had earned him a bad reputation that preceded him wherever he went in Madinah.

Now, taking centre stage, Ibn Salul feigned humility, his hands clasped tightly over his heart. His voice was gentle and steady as he addressed the crowd. "Dear people," he spoke softly, "the Messenger of Allah ﷺ blesses us with his presence. Through him, Allah has bestowed honour upon us. Therefore, it is our duty to support and obey him."

Ibn Salul's kinsmen from the Ansar encircled him with admiration, while the Muhajirun watched with intrigued nods of approval. As the Believers queued up to embrace him, Ibn Salul basked in the blissful felicitations of his supposed conversion to Islam. Alas, beneath his carefully constructed mask, no one detected the demonic smirk that flashed across his face.

Meanwhile, many of the Muhajirun who had migrated from Makkah were feeling homesick. They longed for the familiar climate of their homeland and some had even fallen ill with fever. Aisha couldn't help but worry about her father and the great Companion Bilal, who had both fallen ill upon arriving in Madinah.

Bilal bin Rabah was close to Abu Bakr since he had purchased Bilal's freedom from his cruel master in Makkah.

"O my father, how are you feeling?" Aisha would ask. "And you, O Bilal, how do you fare?"

Abu Bakr would recite couplets of poetry to serve as a reminder:

"Every morning brings family into sight,
But death is nearer than the straps that hold shoes tight."

Bilal, absorbed in memories, would even muse about the plants of Makkah:

"How I wish to spend the night in a valley wide,
Where Idhkhir and Jalil bloom side by side."

Then came the bad news that the Quraysh had seized all the belongings that the Muhajirun had been forced to leave behind in Makkah. Their homes, property and everything that they and their forefathers had built had been stolen. Hearing this, the Prophet ﷺ prayed for his Companions.

"O Allah!" Rasulullah ﷺ said, "Make us love Madinah as much as, or even more than we love Makkah. O Allah! Keep it healthy and bless its *mudd* and *sa'*, and remove its fever, sending it far away to al-Juhfa."

The *mudd* and *sa'* were the traditional measures used for food in Madinah, and his prayer sought blessings for the city's food and harvest.

Madinah
During the lifetime of Aisha رضي الله عنها

Mount Uhud

Mount Sul'

Saqifa Banu Sa'ida

House of Aisha

Masjid Nabawi

Baqi Graveyard

Badr

Masjid Quba

Makkah

CHAPTER 9
Aisha the Bride

For a few years, the Muhajirun lived among their new neighbours, the Ansar of Madinah, slowly getting used to their new home. The Prophet's ﷺ masjid was the beating heart of the community and a beloved place for prayer, learning and meeting people.

But life wasn't easy. The Quraysh had forced the Muslims out of Makkah, taking their homes and stealing everything they left behind - their homes, their belongings and their trade goods. Now, Allah had given His brave Prophet ﷺ permission to fight back and reclaim what was theirs. So, upon hearing that a Quraysh caravan from Makkah, led by their chieftain Abu Sufyan, was passing through the wells of the valley of Badr, the Muslims prepared to confront it.

The Quraysh realised that their caravan was at risk, so they sent a large army to protect it. This led to the Great Battle of Badr, where the Muslims, though far smaller in number and lacking proper weapons, stood their ground with courage and faith. Against all odds, they won a great victory, showing that true strength comes from belief, not just size or weapons. The Prophet ﷺ and his Companions returned to Madinah victorious, their faith strengthened and their enemies shaken.

Aisha's brother, Abdurrahman, had sadly fought on the side of the Quraysh during the Battle of Badr. Aisha missed him desperately, but their family never lost hope that one day he would see the truth and join them.

Back in Madinah, Aisha had blossomed into a young lady and her parents felt that she was ready for married life.

One day, Abu Bakr approached the Prophet ﷺ and asked, "O Messenger of Allah, why don't you bring your wife to live with you in your home now?"

The Prophet's ﷺ response was straightforward. "The dower," he said. Clearly, the Prophet's ﷺ financial situation was not as comfortable as many had assumed. Despite this, he committed himself to providing for his family and ensuring their well-being.

"That's no matter," said Abu Bakr cheerily. "You can borrow money from me." And so, Umm Ruman was summoned to bring Aisha the happy news and prepare her for married life.

Aisha was whisked away by the ladies of the family who brushed her hair, beautified her and brought her lovely dresses to wear. Aisha couldn't believe her eyes when she saw the delightful colours and sumptuous fabrics. She'd never seen such pretty clothing.

"May you bring good fortune!" the women said, erupting in cheers and applause at Aisha's new appearance. The women of the Ansar gathered to serenade the bride. Their voices filled the room with song and laughter as the sound of *duff* drums echoed through Abu Bakr's house.

Dum-di-di-dum-di-di-dum-dum-dum.

They cupped a hand over their mouths and let out an *"Ul-ulululul-leeeee!"*

It was the traditional Arab ululation, a high-pitched trilling sound, made by women to celebrate special occasions. Dressed in their finest robes and adorned with jewellery, the women swayed and chanted in Aisha's honour, their cries of joy and congratulations rising to the sky.

"May Allah bless the union!"

"May her happiness increase!" they cried out, as two friends escorted Aisha in and sat down with her on a plush cushion.

Dum-di-di-dum-di-di-dum-dum-dum.

Dum-di-di-dum-di-di—

Rat-a-tat-tat!

A hush fell over the room as a knock at the door signalled the arrival of the Messenger of Allah ﷺ. Stifled laughter broke out and the girls covered their mouths trying to hide their grins. The beat of the *duff* continued in the background. The ululating faded as the Prophet ﷺ sat down next to Aisha.

Aisha felt as though she was noticing the Prophet's ﷺ appearance properly for the first time. He was of medium height with a complexion that was neither very light nor dark. His black eyes, framed with long eyelashes, sparkled with kindness. His wavy, dark hair cascaded to his broad shoulders.

A bowl of creamy milk appeared and passed from hand to hand until it reached the Prophet ﷺ. When he raised it to his lips, a hush came over the room. He took a sip and offered it to the bride, who blushed and peered at the bowl, her long eyelashes fluttering.

"Take the bowl! Don't turn down his offer!" the ladies said, encouraging Aisha. Asma came forward and gave her sister a helping hand.

The younger girls looked at each other, smirking as Aisha bashfully took the bowl and sipped a little milk.

"Give the milk to your friends," the Prophet ﷺ said, gesturing to the giggling girls.

"Oh, no, no!" the girls insisted. "We have no appetite!"

The Prophet ﷺ gave a knowing smile. "You shouldn't pair hunger with lies!" he remarked.

"O Messenger of Allah," one lady said, "if we say we don't want something, even though we really do, is this considered a lie?"

"Yes," replied the Prophet ﷺ. "An untruth is recorded as a lie. But of course, a little untruth is recorded as a little lie!"

Sa'd bin Ubadah, the leader of the Khazraj tribe, sent a lavish meal to the Prophet ﷺ as a wedding dinner. The warm, comforting aroma of *thareed* wafted through the air and lingered all around. The warm, crisp flatbread, baked to golden perfection, served as the base, while a rich, fragrant sauce, made with spices and herbs, was spooned generously over it. Each bite was a symphony of textures, as the soft bread melted in the mouth, giving way to the delicious meaty sauce.

Elsewhere, deep in the heart of Madinah, Ibn Salul, the conniver, was hatching a plot to take control of the city. His eyes glinted in the dim light of his shadowy chamber as he whispered to his co-conspirators. They became known as the Hypocrites, or *Munafiqun*, because they pretended to be Muslims and acted like Muslims, but didn't really believe in nor follow the Prophet ﷺ.

Ibn Salul paced around his den, plotting and planning, when suddenly a young tribesman slipped into the room. His breath was quick and his eyes darted nervously. "Have you heard?" the young man whispered, his voice shaking with excitement. "The Prophet celebrated his marriage. He builds alliances through marriage with his most noble Companions. Soon, he will build alliances throughout Arabia."

Ibn Salul's lip curled in disgust at the mention of the Prophet's ﷺ name.

"Spare me the news," he snarled, his voice dripping with venom. His bushy eyebrows knotted into a deep scowl and his sharp, hawk-like nose seemed to jut out even further in his fury.

The young man shrank back, cowed by Ibn Salul's menacing demeanour. He knew the leader of the Hypocrites was not to be trifled with, and any misstep could result in dire consequences. With a quick nod of deference, he turned and hurried out of the room, leaving Ibn Salul to his dark designs.

Now that Aisha had crossed the river that separates childhood from womanhood, she was ready to move into her newly built home beside the masjid. Her new house was a simple square-shaped house made from mud bricks with palm leaves for roofing. It was sparsely furnished with only the essentials. Daily tasks like drying clothes or preparing food could be carried out in the *hujrah* which was an open area enclosed by a low fence which even had a door that led straight into the masjid. This *hujrah* could also be used as a place of prayer and quiet reflection, or to keep a goat for fresh milk.

The Prophet's ﷺ wife, Sawdah, an older lady with a kind face, was already living in one of the houses. Sawdah welcomed her blushing new neighbour, who was a vision of loveliness.

The perfumed Prophet ﷺ stepped in and welcomed Aisha to the new home. When she entered the gate, her eyes scanned the little square courtyard outside the house. It was clean and quite roomy, at least big enough to keep some chickens and have a few friends around. The fence around the courtyard was made of long palm leaves. The walls of the house, baked by the scorching desert sun, exuded a rich and earthy aroma.

When she entered her house, her face lit up with excitement. It was a humble home, yet the sunlight streamed through its small window and palm-leaf roof, filling the space with a gentle, welcoming glow. The room was cosy with the ceiling reaching just a little above the Prophet's ﷺ head. The bed featured a leather pillow and a mattress filled with palm fibre. In one corner, a few pots and pans and a large water pitcher rested, while the Prophet's ﷺ wooden staff, long bow, sword and shiny shield lay in another corner. It may have been a small house, but to Aisha, it was her own palace and it was just perfect.

CHAPTER 10
Home Sweet Home

It was Eid day and the Prophet ﷺ appeared all of a sudden through the curtain of black wool, his eyes bright with amusement. He beckoned Aisha to come and see what was happening inside the masjid. He held open the thick curtain that hung over the door that led from their courtyard into the masjid. His broad shoulders shielded Aisha, who stood on tiptoe with her cheek pressed against his. Aisha peeked over the Prophet's ﷺ shoulder.

The Abyssinians, a people renowned for their military prowess, were performing a stunning display in the Prophet's ﷺ masjid. Donning armour that glinted in the light, and wielding weapons that swished and gleamed as they marched in perfect unison, they mesmerised the onlooking crowds.

Aisha's eyes were wide with amazement.

"Whoosh! Swoosh!" went the sharp blades, cutting through the hot Madinan air as they flew. The atmosphere was electric. The graceful Abyssinians demonstrated their battle skills, chanting and moving, filling the air with a rhythmic pulse that resonated through the masjid. The Abyssinians performed a choreographed dance of strength and agility, spinning their spears and shields with breathtaking precision.

Each man stood tall, his arms glowing brown and muscular, his cheekbones high and forehead broad, exuding regal dignity. Aisha noticed the Prophet's ﷺ eyes shining with admiration as he looked on. He held the Abyssinians in high esteem and enjoyed a special relationship with their king, Najashi, who was once a Christian but had secretly embraced Islam. The display came to a close with the Abyssinians standing with their chests puffed out and lowering their spears. The clatter of wood and swishing of metal settled into complete silence as the onlookers erupted into jubilant cheers.

Aisha was a little fatigued after standing for so long to watch the exhilarating performance.

"Are you satisfied?" the Prophet ﷺ whispered, turning to her tenderly. Aisha beamed back at him, nodding vigorously.

Aisha had great affection for her new home. With a small broom in hand, she set about making it a comfortable and inviting space. She swept every nook and cranny, taking care to move quickly from one end of the room to the other. As she worked, Aisha's eyes fell on the corner where she kept the Prophet's ﷺ belongings. A hook on the wall held the Prophet's ﷺ armour, and beside it hung his white shirt and a few other garments. Whenever Aisha walked past his shirt, the glorious, warm scent of musk perfume wafted towards her and she inhaled the wonderful scent.

The Prophet's ﷺ shield, his long bow and heavy sword leaned against the wall, humming with a mysterious energy as if biding their time until they were once again summoned to action by their master. Aisha felt a sense of comfort knowing that she was under the protection of the courageous Prophet ﷺ.

In another corner of the room, Aisha had arranged her food containers and a sack of dates, which were scattered around a collection of clay pots and a woven basket. It was a simple but well-stocked larder, and Aisha took great care to keep it organised and tidy.

One day, Aisha was thinking of giving a gift to her neighbours to brighten up their day. As she was leaving the house, she paused, wondering if she should go left or right. She had so many neighbours now, that her generous little heart was confused about who she should give to. The Prophet's ﷺ daughter, Fatima, and her husband, Ali, had moved into a house on one side, and Sawdah also lived right next to her. So, she returned and asked the Messenger of Allah ﷺ.

"O Messenger of Allah," she said, "I have two neighbours. To whom should I send a gift?"

The Prophet ﷺ looked towards her and said, "To the neighbour who is closest to your front door." So Aisha gifted the neighbour who lived closest to her. Aisha loved to ask the Prophet ﷺ questions, and he entertained every one. His advice always gave her such clarity because, of course, his answers were guided by Allah.

As the leader of the Muslims, the Prophet ﷺ frequently embarked on long and arduous expeditions, bearing the weight of Allah's message on his shoulders. Nevertheless, Aisha never failed to infuse joy and lightness into his life, even amid adversity.

One day, when he had returned from a long expedition, Aisha could see the tiredness in his eyes. As they sat together, catching up on the journey, a sudden gust of wind lifted the corner of a curtain in the room, revealing a collection of what looked like stuffed toys which piqued the Prophet's ﷺ curiosity.

"O Aisha, what is this?" the Prophet ﷺ asked.

"Why, these are my dolls," Aisha replied sheepishly. She'd kept them as they meant so much to her.

One of the objects, the horse with wings fashioned from rags, caught the Prophet's ﷺ eye. "And what is this I see?" he asked.

"A horse," Aisha said.

"And what is that on it?" the Prophet ﷺ pressed further.

"Two wings."

"A horse with two wings?" the Prophet ﷺ repeated, surprised by the very idea.

With her sharp wit, Aisha replied, "Have you not heard that the Prophet Sulayman had horses with two wings?"

The sound of the Prophet's ﷺ laughter echoed through the room, joyfully, and he smiled so broadly that even his molar teeth were visible. The aching tiredness of the journey was gone as they laughed together and recalled stories of the Prophets of the past.

The Prophet ﷺ would divide his time between his wives equally. He loved Aisha's company so much he didn't like to leave her alone on his days with her.

Aisha's home was where delegations would come far and wide to meet the Prophet ﷺ, where widows would seek advice and admirers came to give gifts. The Prophet ﷺ was the leader of Madinah, a statesman, but he helped Aisha with the chores around the house. Aisha, too, took care of the Prophet ﷺ. She would mend his clothes, wash and clean them, comb his beard and rub perfume on her hands, applying it to the Prophet ﷺ before he left for prayer.

One day, there was a knock at the door. It was a servant boy, sent by a Persian neighbour.

"My master has made a delicious soup and invites you, O Messenger of Allah, for a meal."

The Prophet ﷺ looked towards Aisha and then turned to the servant. "And my wife, Aisha?" he asked politely.

The servant indicated that the invitation was only for the Prophet ﷺ. So the Prophet ﷺ respectfully declined the invitation.

The servant went back to his master, who sent him back with the same invite. The Prophet ﷺ once again asked about Aisha. But since she was not invited, he respectfully declined. Then the master understood that the Prophet ﷺ really wanted to bring Aisha along to enjoy the meal and not leave her behind. Thc servant returned a third time, breathless from all the running, and invited both of them to the meal. Together, they made their way to the neighbour's house to enjoy the delightful soup and warm company.

The more Aisha learned from the Prophet ﷺ, the more her love for him grew, and the more she realised the great love he had for his mission and his *Ummah*, the entire Muslim community.

One day, she was lying with her head in the Prophet's ﷺ lap and noticed that he had a cheerful twinkle in his eye. So she said to him eagerly, "O Messenger of Allah, make *du'a* to Allah for me!" She wanted to be blessed with his special prayers just for her.

The Prophet ﷺ said, "O Allah, forgive Aisha for her past and future sins, those done in secret and in public."

Aisha was so overwhelmed by this beautiful and complete *du'a* that she let out a laugh of incredulity. If the Prophet's ﷺ prayer was accepted - and the prayers of Prophets always are - then surely she was destined for Paradise!

Laughing hard, her head slipped from his lap, and the Prophet ﷺ caught her gently in his strong arms. Smiling, he asked softly, "Does my *du'a* make you happy?"

"How could your *du'a* not make me happy?" Aisha replied, giddy with joy.

The Prophet ﷺ smiled again, his eyes shining like polished mirrors, clear and full of serenity. "By Allah," he said gently, "I make this same *du'a* for my Ummah in every single prayer."

CHAPTER 11
A Bond Like No Other

"Go!" And off they dashed, two figures in the desolate, dusky desert, their laughter rising through the air like the scent of wildflowers on a spring breeze. Aisha's nimble feet carried her swiftly, matching the Prophet's ﷺ every stride with determination and grit. The race quickened as they both leaned into their strides, each footfall kicking up the dust behind them. With every leap, Aisha's spirit soared higher, revelling in the thrill of the chase. The world around them faded into insignificance and in that fleeting moment, it was just the two of them, embracing the sheer blissfulness of one another's company.

As the finish drew near, the Prophet ﷺ and Aisha surged forward. In a moment that felt suspended in time, Aisha raced to victory! Her cheeks turned pink as she celebrated her triumph and looked back lovingly at her husband. In his smiling eyes and through their shared adventure, Aisha glimpsed the depth of the Prophet's ﷺ love for her. It was a bond like no other.

O Messenger of Allah," said Aisha one day, "all of my friends have *kunyas*, but I don't. So give me a *kunya* too." A *kunya* was a special nickname given out of respect, that differed from a person's regular name. For men, it began with '*Abu*', meaning 'father of,' and for women, '*Umm*' meaning 'mother of,' and it could be used to name children too. It was usually used to show someone's connection to their child or to reflect a special trait or characteristic they possessed.

Aisha looked up and around the room and realised her little nephew had disappeared. Sighing heavily, she got up and rushed outside the house to see where he could be.

Little Abdullah bin az-Zubayr with his big, curious eyes and tiny hands, explored his aunt Aisha's courtyard. His chubby bare feet sank into the warm sandy ground as he wobbled around, intrigued by the little goat adorned with a coat of pristine white, chewing on a pile of grass in front of him. His aunt Aisha appeared out of the house to see what he was up to and laughed when she saw him trying to compete with the goat for its leafy meal.

The Prophet ﷺ knew how much Aisha loved her nephew Abdullah, so he had a suggestion. "Why not take a *kunya* from your son, Abdullah bin az-Zubayr?" he proposed. Aisha nodded, whisking her nephew up into her arms and cleaning his button-like face. Abdullah was like her son.

Umm Abdillah! She liked the sound of that! From that day on, people sometimes called Aisha 'Umm Abdillah'.

One day, there was a gentle knock at the door. A voice called softly from the other side, "May I enter?"

The Prophet ﷺ looked up from what he was doing and stared at the door. Suddenly, his eyes filled with tears of anguish. It was a familiar voice - a voice he deeply missed. For a moment, his lower lip trembled, and he seemed lost in the grip of emotion.

Then he stood up quickly, remembering the door.

"O Allah! It must be Hala bint Khuwaylid!" he gasped, as he hurried to open it.

Aisha looked on, perplexed by the Prophet's ﷺ raw emotion. There was an elderly lady at the door and when the Prophet ﷺ saw her, it felt as though he had caught a glimpse of Khadijah's familiar face. It was Khadijah's sister, Hala. Although Aisha had never met Khadijah, she knew she had been the Prophet's ﷺ first wife, as he often spoke of her. He never mentioned Khadijah without a catch in his throat.

Meat was an expensive luxury in those days, but when the Prophet ﷺ slaughtered a sheep, he would cut it into pieces and send portions as gifts to each of Khadijah's friends, and seemed to endlessly honour her memory. Aisha felt an ember of jealousy flicker and crackle inside her.

"It is as though there is no woman on Earth except her," Aisha remarked carelessly. "What makes you remember an old woman of the Quraysh so fondly? One who departed from this mortal realm long ago. Hasn't Allah given you in her place a better wife?"

The Prophet ﷺ blinked, dismayed by Aisha's words. He shook his head and flashed a look of disappointment towards her.

"No!" he said with sadness in his voice. "Allah did not give me a better wife than Khadijah. She supported my mission when everybody shouted against it. She believed in me when there was hardly a believer. She enlivened my heart when I felt lonely and deserted. Khadijah's love was gifted to me by Allah. How could I ever forget her?"

Aisha's spirit wilted, her eyes cast downward, drenched in a mixture of remorse and shame. She wished she could take her words back. How foolish she felt! Khadijah must have been an extraordinary woman - not merely beautiful but also blessed with wisdom, since even Allah had honoured her with glad tidings of a palace of pearls in Paradise. She yearned for the Prophet's ﷺ love to embrace her with the same fervour he held for Khadijah and wondered if she would ever be deserving of such reward, or be blessed with wisdom like Khadijah was.

CHAPTER 12
Mother of the Believers

In Arabian society, it was the norm for men to have multiple wives. The Prophet Muhammad ﷺ was already married to Aisha and Sawdah, but now in Madinah, as the leader of the Muslim Ummah, he needed to strengthen the growing Muslim community. During his years in Madinah, he married several wives, many of whom were widows in need of support.

The Prophet ﷺ was a wise leader, just like the Prophets before him. His marriages helped forge relationships with his Companions and build alliances with tribal leaders.

Beyond this, the Prophet's ﷺ marriages carried a powerful message. They showed all Muslim men how important it is to build strong families, taking good care of widows, orphans and women in society.

First, he married Hafsah, the daughter of his Companion Umar bin al-Khattab. Next came Zaynab bint Khuzaymah. Umm Salamah, another widow, joined the household and became a source of wisdom and support. Over the next few years he married a number of other noble ladies. Of them, was his cousin Zainab bint Jahsh and then Juwayriyyah, a woman from the defeated Banu Mustaliq tribe, whose marriage inspired her entire tribe to embrace Islam. After that, Umm Habibah, also known as Ramla, the daughter of Abu Sufyan, a leader of the Quraysh, joined his household. Safiyyah bint Huyayy followed, hailing from a Jewish tribe. Mariyah the Egyptian became the mother of his son, Ibrahim, who sadly passed away as a baby. Lastly, he married Maymunah.

The Prophet ﷺ loved each of the women he married, treating them with respect, kindness and fairness. Each of his wives played a crucial role, contributing to the early Muslim community as role models and nurturers. Allah revealed a verse of the Quran about the status of the Prophet's ﷺ wives as Mothers of the Believers:

"The Prophet is closer to the believers than their own selves, and his wives are their mothers."
(Quran, 33:6)

New houses were built next to the masjid, each assigned to one of the Prophet's ﷺ wives. Every home was an identical small building with a fenced *hujrah*, just like Aisha's.

Aisha, Sawdah and their new co-wife, Hafsah, got on famously. They chatted and laughed like sisters. At night, Aisha would sometimes talk to Hafsah through the shared wall between their houses. Soon the wives had formed two separate groups: one led by Aisha and the other by Umm Salamah.

The Prophet ﷺ gave each of his wives equal time, taking turns and fixing the nights he'd stay with each of them and spending equal amounts of wealth on them. The Prophet ﷺ would enter the house of one of his wives and say, "Peace be upon you! How are you, O members of the household?" He did his best to treat his wives equally and would pray that Allah would help him, saying, "O Allah, I'm doing my best to treat my wives fairly with what I can control. Don't hold me accountable for what You control and I cannot control."

But there was something special about Aisha's house. The atmosphere was often charged with a sense of divine presence, as it was here that revelations would sometimes come to the Prophet ﷺ and verses of the Quran were revealed.

One day, while they were together, the Prophet ﷺ turned to her and said, "O Aisha, here is the Angel Jibreel to greet you with peace." Aisha looked around but could not see the angel.

She felt honoured and replied, "And upon him be peace, the mercy of Allah, and His blessings. You see what I do not see!"

Deep within the depths of Aisha's heart, a silent struggle unfolded. Though she shared moments of friendship with her co-wives, there were occasions when she had to fight back the overwhelming intensity of her emotions. She was still young and yearned to be the Prophet's ﷺ most beloved wife, dreading the thought of being overshadowed by another. Yet, her faith urged her to maintain her dignity and grace as a believing woman. Sometimes it wasn't so easy.

CHAPTER 13
The Choice

In the presence of Angel Jibreel, Rasulullah ﷺ lifted his eyes to the heavens and saw a radiant figure descending from the celestial realm.

"Behold!" Angel Jibreel whispered. "This angel has not graced our Earth since the dawn of time." The Prophet ﷺ, wide-eyed and dazzled, watched as the new angel approached.

"O Muhammad," the angel spoke with a firm voice. "Your Lord has sent me to offer you a choice: to rule as a Prophet-king or to live as a servant-Messenger."

Angel Jibreel urged the Prophet ﷺ, "Be humble before the Almighty, O Muhammad." The Prophet ﷺ nodded with

understanding. "I choose to be a servant-Messenger," he replied.

From that day on, the Prophet ﷺ embraced a life of simplicity, eating little and showing gratitude for the smallest blessings from Allah. He insisted that his wives also live the same way, detached from the pleasures of this world, focusing instead on the eternal reward of the life hereafter.

This way of life was difficult for the wives of the Prophet ﷺ. There were times when days would pass without a cooked meal and they would live on nothing but dates and water. The hardship took its toll and the wives started sending their complaints to the Prophet ﷺ, telling him that this lifestyle was becoming too hard for them to bear.

One day, Umar had an argument with his wife and scolded her for speaking back to him. His wife, unfazed, replied, "Why do you get upset when I respond to you? By Allah, even the wives of the Prophet ﷺ sometimes speak back to him. There are times when some of them do not speak to him the entire day until night."

Umar couldn't believe his ears. He shuddered at the thought of his own daughter, Hafsah, answering back to the Messenger of Allah ﷺ. Without delay, he got dressed and hurried to Hafsah's home.

"Is it true?" Umar asked her, his voice stern. "Do some of you argue with the Messenger of Allah ﷺ in such a way that he is upset for an entire day?" Hafsah looked down, nodding sheepishly.

"Then you are ruined!" Umar exclaimed in alarm. "Do you not fear Allah? Don't you realise that upsetting the Prophet ﷺ could bring Allah's anger and cause your ruin?" Hafsah sniffed, unable to find the words to respond, her heart heavy with her father's warning. "Make no mistake, Hafsah," Umar said bluntly, "your neighbour may get away with what you cannot. For she is more beautiful and more beloved to the Messenger of Allah ﷺ than you." He pointed toward Aisha's house as he spoke. Hafsah stood there, speechless. Deep down, she knew her father was right.

"Listen to me," Umar continued, his tone softening. "Anything you need, ask me for it. Stop asking the Messenger of Allah ﷺ for things." Hafsah nodded, feeling the weight of her father's words sink in.

Umar stopped by Umm Salamah's house too, as he was one of her relatives. However, Umm Salamah found his line of questioning uncomfortable. "O son of al-Khattab," she exclaimed. "It is quite astonishing that you would even interfere between Allah's Messenger ﷺ and his wives!" She then reassured him that there was nothing to worry about.

Meanwhile, in Aisha's household, a similar storm was brewing. Abu Bakr came to visit the Prophet ﷺ, only to hear Aisha's voice raised in conversation. Upon entering, Abu Bakr was visibly upset and approached Aisha to rebuke her for raising her voice in front of the Prophet ﷺ. But before he could act, the Prophet ﷺ stepped in, shielding Aisha who rushed to hide behind him. In a calm manner, he diffused the situation. Abu Bakr still felt frustrated and decided to leave. After he left, the Prophet ﷺ turned to Aisha with a playful smile and said, "Did you see how I protected you from that man?"

Allah had granted the Prophet's ﷺ wives some leniency - allowing room for natural emotions and occasional disputes - recognising the special bond they shared with the Prophet ﷺ and knowing that, like every marriage, there were bound to be ups and downs.

A few days later, when Abu Bakr returned for a visit, Aisha and the Prophet ﷺ had made peace. Seeing them happy, Abu Bakr remarked, "Won't you include me in your peace, just as I was part of your disagreement?"

With a warm smile, the Prophet ﷺ replied, "We already have! We already have!"

Aisha and Hafsah sat in Hafsah's house, looking glum. This time, they had gone too far.

The Prophet ﷺ started going to Zaynab's house daily to enjoy a delicious drink that Zaynab would make from honey. Aisha and Hafsah noticed this routine and felt rather jealous.

The Prophet ﷺ always smelled heavenly. He avoided eating things that left an unpleasant smell, like onion and garlic. People observed that he always smelled of the most exquisite musk.

Aisha and Hafsah decided to stop the Prophet ﷺ from his visits to Zaynab's house by playing a little prank. When the Prophet ﷺ came to them after visiting Zaynab, they would tell him they could smell something strange from him.

"What is that smell?" Aisha asked. "Did you eat some *maghafir?" Maghafir* was a foul-smelling fruit.

The Prophet ﷺ looked surprised. "I have just drunk some honey," he said.

Later, when he visited Hafsah, the same thing happened.

"What is that smell?" Hafsah asked, "Did you eat some *maghafir?*"

"No, but I have drunk honey in the house of Zaynab bint Jahsh," he said. Now the Prophet ﷺ was mortified at the thought of two of his wives complaining of the same unpleasant smell. "I vow never to drink the honey drink ever again."

But Allah revealed verses of the Quran which informed him of their trick and told him not to vow to avoid the things that Allah had made lawful for him:

> *"O Prophet! Why do you prohibit yourself from what Allah has made lawful to you, seeking to please your wives? And Allah is All-Forgiving, Most Merciful."*
>
> (Quran, 66:3)

Allah also revealed a verse telling the wives of the Prophet ﷺ not to take their position for granted. For if Allah wanted, he could replace them all.

Aisha and Hafsah were full of remorse and wished they could disappear for a while. The other wives looked on at Aisha and Hafsah with disapproval. They were not amused.

The Messenger of Allah ﷺ was an exceptionally patient man and handled his wives' behaviour with good humour. However, the recent demands and the squabbling were becoming all too much for him. The

Prophet ﷺ was an important man, with important work to do. He needed his wives to support his work and understand that as a Prophet, he had to set the best example of living a simple, unworldly life. He needed space to think, and his wives needed time to reflect on their behaviour. So, the Prophet ﷺ retreated to his granary, a small loft for storing supplies he could access by climbing a ladder from one of his houses, and stayed there for a month.

BANG! BANG! BANG!

There was a loud, hard knocking on Umar's door. Worry washed over him as he creaked the door open.

"What is it?" he gasped. "Has the Ghassan tribe attacked us?"

"It is more serious than that, O Umar!" came the reply. "It appears the Messenger of Allah ﷺ has divorced his wives!"

"What? Then Hafsah is ruined!" Umar roared, hurriedly pulling on his clothes. Without wasting a moment, he made his way to the masjid for *Fajr*, where he joined the Prophet ﷺ in prayer.

The Messenger of Allah ﷺ said nothing about the matter and retreated to the granary. Observing this, Umar headed towards Hafsah's house. When he arrived, he found Hafsah in tears.

"Why are you weeping?" he scolded. "Didn't I warn you, Hafsah? Has Rasulullah ﷺ divorced you all?"

"I don't know," cried Hafsah. "He is in the granary."

Umar sighed and made his way to the loft room, where the Prophet's ﷺ servant was sitting by the entrance. "Could you please ask the Prophet ﷺ for permission for Umar to enter?" He paced back and forth outside the entrance. The servant went inside for a while and then came back.

"I mentioned you to him, but he didn't respond," the servant said. Umar nodded and went to sit in the masjid with the other worshippers. However, a few minutes later, he sprang up again, unable to bear the uncertainty any longer.

"Please, ask for my permission to enter once more," Umar said to the servant. Once again, the servant disappeared, only to return with the same reply. Frustrated, Umar stood up to leave. Just as he was about to exit, the servant-boy called out his name.

"Allah's Messenger ﷺ has granted you permission!" he said, panting. Umar was elated and entered the Prophet's ﷺ granary, bending his neck in order to enter it. It was a small room with only a rough mat on the ground, upon which the Prophet ﷺ lay. When the Prophet ﷺ sat up, Umar noticed the marks all over his body from the rough fibres of the mat. The only other items in the room were the Prophet's ﷺ leather cushion, which was stuffed with palm fibres, and a small bag of barley and another of acacia pods.

Umar stayed standing and lowered his eyes in the Prophet's ﷺ presence, greeting him.

"Have you... er... divorced your wives, O Messenger of Allah ﷺ?" Umar asked tentatively, his heart almost stopping.

"No," the Prophet ﷺ responded. Umar began breathing again and was visibly relieved.

"Do you know, O Messenger of Allah," Umar began, raising his eyebrows as he spoke, "the problem, as I see it, is that we, the people of Quraysh, have always had the upper hand over our women. But here in Madinah, we've found that the women have taken charge over their men." He continued, explaining how their wives had been deeply influenced by this new way of life, and how the dynamics between husbands and wives were shifting in ways he never foresaw.

The Prophet's ﷺ face broke into a smile.

"What's more, I went to Hafsah and told her 'Do not be tempted to imitate your co-wife, Aisha, for she is more beautiful than you and more beloved to the Prophet'."

The Prophet ﷺ couldn't help but smile again.

Seeing the Prophet ﷺ relaxed and in good spirits, Umar sat down. As he glanced around the room and into the eyes of the man for whom he would willingly lay down his life, tears welled up in his own. Here he was, in the presence of the greatest man on Earth - yet there were no crowns, no thrones, no pomp and circumstance.

"What is making you weep, O Ibn al-Khattab?" the Prophet ﷺ asked, noticing the tears in Umar's eyes.

"O Prophet of Allah," Umar said, "how can I not weep when I see the marks this mat has left on your side? In your granary, there is nothing but what I can see. Meanwhile, Caesar and Khosrow indulge in endless fruits and rivers, and you are the Messenger of Allah, His chosen one." He looked down, his voice heavy with emotion.

"Plead with Allah," Umar continued, "to enrich your Ummah like the Persians and Byzantines are enriched. They bask in unimaginable prosperity and worldly luxuries, even though they do not worship Allah."

At that, the Prophet ﷺ sat up straight, his tone growing serious.

"O Ibn al-Khattab!" he said, "Aren't you satisfied that we have the Hereafter while they possess only this life?"

Umar nodded. "Yes," he replied, recalling that what Allah had prepared for the Believers in the Hereafter was far greater and more magnificent. "Please seek forgiveness for me from Allah," he added.

On the final day of the month, the Prophet ﷺ emerged from his room and went to Aisha's house. "I have a message for you," he said gently, "but don't rush to respond until you've consulted your parents."

Allah had commanded the Prophet ﷺ to give his wives a choice. If they found life as his wives too difficult, they were free to leave and seek happiness elsewhere. However, if they wished to remain, they would share in the great responsibilities and blessings of being Mothers of the Believers. They would need to exercise patience, but they would also be rewarded handsomely by Allah.

The Prophet ﷺ recited the words of Allah to Aisha:

> *"O Prophet! Say to your wives, 'If you desire the life of this world and its luxury, then come, I will give you a suitable compensation, and let you go graciously. But if you desire Allah and His Messenger and the everlasting home of the Hereafter, then surely Allah has prepared a great reward for those of you who do good'."*
>
> (Quran, 33:28-29)

Upon hearing these verses, Aisha's eyes widened with conviction. "Do I really need to consult my parents about this?" she exclaimed, incredulous. "Without a doubt, I choose Allah, His Messenger, and the Hereafter!"

The Prophet ﷺ offered the same choice to his other wives. They responded with the same unwavering commitment as Aisha.

CHAPTER 14
The Dignity of Hijab

In the vibrant city of Madinah, the women embraced the fashion of their time, adorning themselves with garments that reflected the customs of Arab culture. Some wore long, elegant dresses with delicate headdresses or scarves to cover their hair, while others chose loose, flowing pantaloons paired with tunics and stylish headdresses. They exposed their necks or hair, and adorned themselves with jewellery and decorative garments. These were all visible. Madinah was a mixed society, with Believers and Disbelievers, and of course, the dreaded Hypocrites who always looked for opportunities to cause trouble.

Allah had made it the duty of men to look after women. They were equal in value in Allah's eyes, however, they were not the same. Their roles complemented each other. Allah had also made women especially precious. Their beauty was a wonderful gift and was to be displayed at the right time and with the right people.

But through the bustling streets of the city, a change was about to unfold. In His infinite wisdom, Allah revealed verses in the Quran, instructing both men and women to lower their gazes and guard their eyes from looking at inappropriate things.

He then provided further commands for the believing men and women to follow. For the believing women, Allah gave new laws for when they left their homes:

> *"O Prophet! Tell your wives and your daughters and the women of the Believers to draw their cloaks (jilbabs) all over their bodies. That will be better, that they should be recognised and not be harmed. And Allah is Ever Oft-Forgiving, Most Merciful."*
>
> (Quran, 33:59)

Allah revealed verses in the Quran about women's outer garments, instructing the believing women to cover themselves when they go outside. These dignified garments should be loose and not see-through and should cover their bodies so as not to show off their beauty and jewellery. They were not to expose anything of their bodies in front of men, unless they were their *mahrams*. *Mahrams* are men who are closely related to a woman in such a way that she can't marry them, like brothers, fathers, grandfathers, nephews and certain uncles. Allah also revealed verses telling the women to use their headscarves to cover their hair, necks and ears fully, and to cover their chests:

> *"Let them let their headscarves (khimars) cover over their chests, and not reveal their hidden adornments..."*
> (Quran, 24:31)

This instruction was given so that the Muslim women would be recognised as such and treated with respect, whoever they interacted with. This way of dressing allowed Muslim women to go about their daily lives, focusing on their activities without attracting unwanted attention or being treated as objects of desire. It would also remind the women themselves to keep a sense of decorum about themselves in public, and in the presence of men who weren't closely related to them.

As soon as the verses of hijab were revealed, the Prophet ﷺ recited them to the people in the masjid and they went home and told their wives and daughters. The women of Madinah said, "We hear and we obey!" They took the extra fabric they had at home and began making cloaks as outer garments to cover themselves, just as they had been commanded.

The Muslim women knew that by dressing this way in public, they were obeying Allah's command. When people saw them, they'd know that they were Muslim women. It gave people the message: what stands before you is a Believing woman. A woman who knows her worth, who has enormous strength and integrity, and who wants to obey Allah. She is not an object or plaything, as some societies might treat her.

In those days, there were no bathrooms attached to people's houses. People travelled out into the desert to answer the call of nature. One day, when Umar was walking outside, he recognised Sawdah, the wife of the Prophet ﷺ, going out for her needs.

"I have recognised you, O Sawdah!" Umar said, feeling uncomfortable on her behalf.

People shouldn't be able to notice the wives of the Prophet so easily, he thought. *They are far too special.*

Umar wrestled with his thoughts and decided he would bring up his concerns with the Messenger of Allah ﷺ. However, when Sawdah told the Prophet ﷺ, he reassured her that if the women dressed properly, there was nothing wrong with them going out.

"Allah has given permission to you to go out for your needs," he explained. The Prophet ﷺ also instructed the men, saying, "Do not prevent the female servants of Allah from going to the masjids of Allah, but they should go out without wearing perfume." In this way, a beautiful balance was struck. Women were free to attend the masjid and fulfil their spiritual needs, but they were reminded to avoid anything that might draw attention, such as perfume and ornaments. This ensured that the sacred space of the masjid remained focused on worship and devotion to Allah.

The hijab was akin to an honourable crown adorning Muslim women, a demonstration of faith and obedience to Allah's command. They felt their beauty was protected, recognising the value of preserving precious things instead of flaunting them.

Aisha and the Believing women didn't hesitate to obey Allah. They knew that anything that Allah commanded them with was for their own good, and anything Allah forbade them from was harmful to them and to society. For Allah is All-Wise, and He knows His creation better than we know ourselves, guiding us with perfect wisdom.

CHAPTER 15
Curtains and Shattered Plates

At the entrance of the Prophet's ﷺ dwelling, Umar stood tall and commanding. His serious expression mirrored the weight of his thoughts. With a frowning eye, he scanned the line of men, some local, many from outside Madinah, who eagerly awaited their turn to visit the Prophet ﷺ. With his fingers tracing the bristles of his beard, Umar felt a restless unease stirring within him.

The Prophet Muhammad ﷺ was a statesman and had visitors who came to resolve their disputes, to seek his advice and guidance, and to negotiate with him. One by one, delegations and visitors would seek permission, and once the Prophet ﷺ permitted them to enter, they'd sit, seek advice and often stay to eat a meal. Umar noticed that the wives of the Prophet ﷺ, including his daughter Hafsah, seemed uncomfortable in the small space in which they dwelled, especially when there were men around. It was clear that they needed more privacy. With every stroke of his beard, he became more and more convinced of it.

"O Messenger of Allah," Umar said, his tone filled with deep respect. "In your noble home, both the virtuous and the sinners find solace. Would it not be fitting when they visit, to advise the Mothers of the Believers to veil themselves behind a curtain?"

Now, it was around the time when the Prophet ﷺ married Zaynab bint Jahsh that some special rules were revealed for the Mothers of the Believers. Anas bin Malik, the devoted teenage Companion and servant of the Prophet ﷺ, was enjoying a tranquil evening. The sun had dipped below the horizon, casting a warm golden glow over the peaceful streets of Madinah. Anas made his way towards a gathering of the Sahaba. They had sought him out, eager to hear his firsthand account of the events that unfolded in Zaynab's house earlier that day.

"Tell us, O Anas, what happened with the Prophet in Zaynab's house today?" the Companions eagerly requested. Anas paused for a moment, collecting his thoughts as he narrated the significant moments of that day. The older men gathered around him, eager to hear his account.

"A banquet of bread and meat was held to celebrate the marriage of the Prophet to Zaynab bint Jahsh," Anas recalled. "I was sent to invite the people to partake in the banquet and so the people started coming in groups. They would eat and then leave. Another batch would come, eat and leave. So I kept on inviting the people till I found nobody to invite."

He then described how the Prophet ﷺ went out and visited Aisha, and the other wives' homes. When he returned, people were still sitting and talking in his house and he was too kind to tell them they were inconveniencing him. It was then that the verses of the Quran were revealed:

> *"O you who believe! Do not enter the houses of the Prophet unless permission is given to you for a meal... and when you ask his wives for something, ask them from behind a screen."*
> (Quran, 33:53)

So the Prophet ﷺ drew a curtain to separate Zaynab from the guests, including from Anas himself, who was a young adult man. The men understood the significance of this action. It signified the special status held by the wives as the Mothers of the Believers. From that day forward, the wives of the Prophet ﷺ observed a particular form of hijab, where men who were not their close relatives could only converse with them from behind a screen or curtain.

Aisha was meticulous from that day forth, to cover herself fully whenever she needed to leave the house. She would wear a *jilbab*, a long outer garment, and when men walked past them, Aisha and the Mothers of the Believers would cover their faces, leaving just a little gap to see through. And when the men had gone, Aisha and the Mothers of the Believers would uncover their faces again. When Aisha was inside her home, and there were male visitors present who were not related to her, she would only speak to them from behind her curtain.

As for Umar, when he heard about the special verse of hijab, he could only smile with satisfaction. Divine revelation proved his gut feeling right.

Now, Aisha thought that Zaynab bint Jahsh was particularly beautiful and had heard that Allah had instructed the Prophet ﷺ to marry her through verses revealed in the Quran. Zaynab, like Aisha, came from noble ancestry; her mother was the Prophet's ﷺ aunt.

Sometimes Zaynab would boast to the other wives when they compared their virtues. "Your families arranged your marriages, but it was Allah who arranged my marriage from above the seven heavens!"

Aisha and Zaynab competed to win the Prophet's ﷺ favour, and the rivalry grew even stronger because Zaynab was part of Umm Salamah's group within the household and not Aisha's.

Once, on Aisha's designated day, the Prophet ﷺ was at her house with a guest when there was a knock at the door. A messenger stood outside, presenting a beautifully crafted dish brimming with delicious food. Aisha's eyes locked onto the dish, recognising that it came from Zaynab's home.

Young Aisha's mind flooded with all sorts of thoughts. Was Zaynab attempting to win the Prophet's ﷺ favour? Without thinking, and in a moment of frustration, Aisha struck the servant's hands, causing the dish to slip from his grasp and clatter and shatter into countless pieces. Gasps filled the air as everyone gazed at the fragments of the broken dish scattered on the ground. Then a hush descended as they paused, speechless.

The Prophet ﷺ knelt and gathered the pieces of cracked pottery and salvaged the pieces of food. He then directed the servant to retrieve a dish from Aisha's own pantry, to be offered as compensation to Zaynab. Aisha could only blush with embarrassment at her outburst in the presence of the Prophet's ﷺ guests.

"Your mother became a little jealous," the Prophet ﷺ remarked, to excuse Aisha's indiscretion, and a gentle smile graced his blessed lips.

CHAPTER 16
She is Abu Bakr's Daughter

The people of Madinah understood Aisha's special place in the Prophet's ﷺ heart, so they would come bearing gifts and food on the days they knew he would be staying with her.

Why do the gifts always arrive on Aisha's day? The other wives wondered. *Why not on any other day?* Some of them couldn't help but feel it was unfair. Naturally, the Messenger of Allah ﷺ had no control over when people chose to give gifts. Yet, despite the good intentions behind these gestures, they stirred feelings of discontent among the other wives.

So, Umm Salamah's group of wives addressed the issue and asked the Messenger of Allah ﷺ to tell the people to send their gifts to him in whichever wife's house he was. With determination, Umm Salamah took the lead and went to the Prophet ﷺ.

When the Prophet ﷺ heard their request, he did not reply. It was not in his character to ask people for gifts or to expect them, let alone to dictate when they should or shouldn't give them.

"He didn't say anything," Umm Salamah reported. The wives urged her to ask again, so she pressed him once more.

"Do not upset me in relation to Aisha," the Prophet ﷺ finally said. "For Allah only sends me His revelation when I am in her home and not with any of the other wives."

Umm Salamah, a God-fearing woman, felt a wave of remorse. "I repent to Allah for upsetting you," she said. She realised the Prophet ﷺ was telling her such gifts and other blessings were not within his control. They were special blessings from Allah for Aisha, and Allah chooses whomever He wills to receive His blessings.

Certain wives then asked the Prophet's ﷺ beloved daughter, Fatima, to speak to him on their behalf about their concerns. Fatima delivered their message, and the Prophet ﷺ said to her, "My daughter, don't you love what I love?"

She answered, "Yes," and decided not to broach the subject again.

The complaints grew too loud to ignore, and one day, Zaynab confronted Aisha in front of the Prophet ﷺ, raising her voice with sharp words. Aisha glanced at the Prophet's ﷺ face for guidance, wondering if she could respond. Realising that she could, Aisha answered Zaynab, giving as good as she got until Zaynab was left speechless. The Prophet ﷺ watched her strong response with a blend of disbelief and amusement. "She truly is the daughter of Abu Bakr!" he finally said.

CHAPTER 17
The Onyx Necklace

Aisha's heart was filled with excitement as she heard the news. The Prophet ﷺ had drawn lots to determine which of his wives would join him on the next expedition, and on this occasion, the lot had fallen in her favour.

Drawing lots was a way to make decisions fairly, leaving the outcome to Allah. They marked small pebbles or datestones and assigned each person a specific object. Then the stones were put into a bag and shaken. A person was given the job of drawing the lots and would reach into the bag and pick one out at random. This time, Aisha's stone had been drawn.

The tension in Madinah had been rising. News had spread that the Banu Mustaliq were gathering forces, possibly planning an attack against the Muslims. The Banu Mustaliq, a powerful tribe allied with the Quraysh, were preparing near a water source called Al-Muraysi. They hoped to launch a surprise attack on Madinah and crush the growing Muslim community. To protect the Muslims and prevent bloodshed inside the city, the ever-watchful Prophet ﷺ, decided to lead a swift expedition to confront them before the threat could grow.

No one knew for certain whether there would be a battle, but they had to be prepared. The men carried their weapons, their faces set with quiet resolve as they braced for the unknown.

Aisha gathered her essentials for the journey in a whirlwind of anticipation. She recognised the seriousness of the journey, but a spark of excitement still danced within her. Since she loved to dress well for her husband, she picked up one of her favourite accessories from her sister Asma. Going on a journey, one that could result in a battle or skirmish, was hardly the time or place to dress up. She hesitated, then tucked the treasured onyx necklace into her pocket as she stepped out of her door.

Aisha gazed at the necklace, holding it up to the sunlight. The glossy, deep-black onyx beads reflected the light, creating a stark contrast against her fair skin. Each bead had its own unique charm as if it held secrets from distant lands.

She couldn't help but wonder about the incredible journey these beads had taken to find their way to her. Maybe they had travelled all the way from Yemen, the land of fragrant *luban* - frankincense. Or perhaps they had come from Persia, the realm of the magnificent palaces of Khosrow. She even imagined they might have come from al-Hind, India, which was known as a land of vibrant colours, tantalising spices and rich traditions. The possibilities seemed endless, and the thought of these beads carrying a piece of history from faraway lands excited her imagination.

Draped in her *jilbab*, the flowing outer garment that enveloped her entire body, Aisha covered her face modestly whenever men passed by. At the departure station, a magnificent camel stood tall, its presence commanding attention. Adjacent to the camel, resting upon the ground, was a *hawdaj* - an extraordinary contraption resembling a miniature tented room, supported by sturdy sticks. Her trusty camel, a vital companion in the harsh and unforgiving terrain they were about to travel through, knelt obediently under the guidance of the camel driver.

Aisha opened the curtain of the *hawdaj* and gracefully climbed into it. Inside, the *hawdaj* had a seat, offering just enough room for her to sit or recline, which was not much room at all. Soft rays of sunlight filtered through the front opening, which Aisha could open or close as desired, allowing her to control the amount of light within, and giving her the chance to relax and take off some of her outer garments.

Four strong men lifted up Aisha's *hawdaj* onto the camel. She was so light, they could hardly tell if she was inside. Although the camel was sitting down, its enormous hump was rather high up. The *hawdaj* wobbled a little until they got it into the perfect position and secured it with ropes under the camel.

Positioned on either side of the camel were water skins, clothes and provisions, neatly bundled up and secured. Soon, the expedition to Banu Mustaliq would commence. It promised to be a lengthy and uncertain journey, but Aisha nevertheless felt immense joy accompanying the Prophet ﷺ and was determined to assist throughout their travels.

In times of battles or expeditions, the women accompanying the troops would set up tents to nurse the wounded, provide water to the soldiers and offer words of encouragement to the brave warriors. It was hard work. On this journey, they didn't know what to expect.

The infinite horizon stretched out before Aisha like an ocean of sand and was both captivating and daunting. As the caravan traversed the vast desert, the sun began its descent, signalling nightfall. The weary travellers halted and pitched their tents, glad for some respite from the scorching sun and the ceaseless winds.

"We must resume our journey at dawn," called out the caravan guide, urging everyone to rest.

The Prophet ﷺ and Aisha had walked to a secluded area where they couldn't be seen. They exchanged glances, realising it was the perfect spot for a race. This would be easy, Aisha thought, remembering the previous race she had won. But that was a long time ago, and she had grown quite a lot since then. This time, the Prophet ﷺ won the race!

"You outran me!" Aisha exclaimed, gasping for breath.

"Today's race is for that race!" the Prophet ﷺ responded.

As the first rays of dawn streaked the horizon, painting the sky with hues of gold and orange, Aisha meticulously inspected her belongings, ensuring that everything was

CHAPTER 17

packed and accounted for. As the time for departure approached, her fingers reached for her neck, only to discover there was nothing there.

"O Rasulullah," she exclaimed with alarm in her voice. "My sister's necklace is missing!"

The Prophet ﷺ instructed the group to pause and search for Aisha's misplaced necklace. Each member scoured the surroundings, combing the area diligently, yet it was nowhere to be found.

The time for the end of morning prayer loomed closer and soon the sun would peek above the horizon. But there was no water in sight for them to make *wudu*! The caravan had relied on reaching an oasis before sunrise to fulfil their prayers, but now it looked like they would miss it.

"Abu Bakr's daughter has caused us this predicament," murmured the restless crowd, their frustration echoing through the camp. The murmurings reached Abu Bakr's ears, and he headed with a furrowed brow towards his daughter's tent.

Upon entering, Abu Bakr discovered the Prophet of Allah ﷺ taking a nap, his head cradled in Aisha's lap. His gaze sharpened as it fell upon his daughter. Aisha turned her head sheepishly, casting furtive glances at her father from the corner of her eye. Abu Bakr's expression grew stern, annoyed at his daughter.

"You have delayed Allah's Messenger ﷺ and the people while there is no water here, nor any water left!" Abu Bakr chided, delivering a firm poke to her thigh for her carelessness. Aisha felt a wave of sorrow wash over her, but she didn't dare move. She didn't want to disturb her napping husband. Abu Bakr shook his head and left.

Meanwhile, the rest of the camp grew increasingly vexed. How would they perform their prayers without water for ablution? Would they be held accountable for missing their sacred obligation?

Just as despair began to settle, a moment of divine intervention unfolded. Allah, in His infinite mercy, revealed verses of the Quran to the Prophet Muhammad ﷺ:

"And if you are ill, or on a journey, or one of you comes from the place of relieving themselves, or have been intimate with your wives, and you find no water, then perform the Tayammum by rubbing your hands with clean earth and wiping over your faces and your hands. And Allah is Most-Pardoning, Most Forgiving."
(Quran, 4:43)

A collective sense of relief resonated through the camp as the verse of *tayammum* - the dry ablution - was revealed.

Abu Bakr had been pacing, lost in thought, when a man approached him, smiling from ear to ear. Now what could there possibly be to smile about?

"Abu Bakr! This is not the first gift that your family has given to Islam!" Abu Bakr was perplexed. The Muslims erupted in joyous exclamations of "*Alhamdulillah*!" - praise be to Allah.

Tayammum, the act of performing dry ablution using clean earth, had been granted as a concession and blessing for Muslims until the end of time. Whether they were travelling or facing dire circumstances without water, they could pat their hands on sand, or stone, or any clean earth material and wipe their faces and hands, and this would be their ablution. This meant they could fulfil their prayers anywhere, even when they had no water.

Abu Bakr made his way back to Aisha's tent, his spirits lifted. "My darling daughter," he addressed her with a touch of remorse, "I could never have fathomed that you would be the source of such a profound blessing. Through you, the Muslims have been granted this concession."

Aisha beamed, a mixture of relief and joy illuminating her face. As the caravan prepared to resume their journey and Aisha's camel rose to its feet, a sudden cry rang out.

"There it is! The onyx necklace!" exclaimed a member of the group. It had been nestled beneath Aisha's camel all along.

CHAPTER 18
Enemies Conspire

The Muslim army had set up camp by the water of al-Muraysi. Aisha stayed with the other women behind the lines, preparing cloth and water in case the wounded needed tending. Sheltered inside her tent, she caught the faint sounds of shouts and the quick, sharp ring of metal on metal - but the fighting was brief, barely more than a skirmish. News soon spread through the camp that the Muslims had been victorious. As the camp began to break apart and the caravan prepared to move on, Aisha sensed that not everyone was at ease, though she could not yet know why.

Ibn Salul was in his grand tent, at a considerable distance from the rest of the caravan. As he sat on a plush cushion, an emergency session was in progress with his conniving cabal of conspirators. Next to him was a young boy, Zayd bin Arqam, and every so often, he'd pat the lad's head as though he were a treasured pet. Zayd gazed up innocently at the uncles around him, each face etched with lines of discontent. They sat in a semicircle, their piercing glares betraying the anger simmering within their souls.

Earlier in the journey, a heated argument had erupted between the Muhajirun and the Ansar, reviving long-forgotten feuds. Swords teetered on the brink of being unsheathed. The Prophet ﷺ, keen to banish their tribalism, had intervened and, with extraordinary skill, calmed the brewing storm, reminding them of their brotherhood.

Rumour had it that Ibn Salul and the Hypocrites had instigated the trouble. Now that it had been quelled, Ibn Salul was seething with fury.

"You fools! You allowed the Muhajirun to gain the whip hand over you! You were once a tribe of great superiority, and now you are outnumbered in your own land because of your feeble, tender hearts! Feed a dog, and it will surely devour you! The wisdom of the ancients holds true regarding us and these vagabonds!"

Little Zayd's eyes widened with alarm as Ibn Salul's heavy hand once again descended upon his head, ruffling his hair in the process.

"By Allah, when we return to Madinah," he hissed, pointing his index finger in the air. "The elite among us will cast out the lowly ones. Yes, the Muhajirun and their Prophet will be expelled! Out! All of them out!" Ibn Salul declared.

Zayd's throat tightened with apprehension as the men erupted into laughter, exchanging hearty slaps on their backs. Each burst of laughter cast long shadows, dancing menacingly on the canvas walls of the tent. The men's faces became obscured in the dim light, their features a collage of dark eyes and gleaming teeth, with the occasional glint of gold from a tooth or a ring. Zayd's wide eyes scanned the tent, waiting for the right moment. And through the laughter and din, the men didn't notice little Zayd's feet barely whispering against the sandy floor, his nimble fingers lifting the edge of the tent flap, just enough for him to slip out and vanish.

After Zayd recounted to the Messenger of Allah ﷺ what he had witnessed in Ibn Salul's tent, the attending Companions exchanged knowing looks and silently shook their heads.

"Treason!" one of the Companions declared.

"It is clear mutiny," another said.

The Muslims had witnessed too much treachery from Ibn Salul to bear it any more. He was like a secret agent, a spy, operating in their midst and informing their enemies of their every move. He had allied with their enemies against them in previous battles and tried to instigate rebellion among the Muslim soldiers. He never failed to snipe at the Messenger of Allah ﷺ when he got a chance, with an insult or snide remark. And now this?

"Have Abbad execute him," Umar declared nonchalantly, motioning towards the sturdy and brave Companion, Abbad bin Bishr. A capable military leader, Abbad always stood ready to protect the Messenger of Allah ﷺ.

"No," the Prophet ﷺ replied firmly. "People will say, 'Muhammad slays his own Companions'." He paused to let the gravity of his words sink in. "Instead, give the command to prepare for departure," he declared.

"But it is an inconvenient time for travel," one of the Companions objected. The Prophet ﷺ insisted, and the men scattered, spreading the call for the caravan to gather their belongings, load their camels and continue the journey back to Madinah.

A thunderous voice from outside the tent broke the calm of their thoughts. It was Ibn Salul accompanied by a group from the Ansar. Those inside the tent began to leave, their frosty stares cutting through Ibn Salul with icy intensity.

Ibn Salul pretended not to notice and launched into his staged defence. "I do bear witness that you are indeed the Messenger of Allah!" he protested. "Never did I utter a word against you! How is that conceivable?" he exclaimed passionately.

The Ansari men with him quickly stepped in to defend him.

"Perhaps young Zayd misunderstood," they said. "He may not have fully grasped what he heard."

The Prophet ﷺ graciously accepted their excuse and calmly instructed them to prepare for departure. It was time to move on to the next stop in their long journey home - just one more stage before they would finally reach Madinah.

Aisha peeked out of her tent with anxious eyes. The crier's voice echoed urgently, announcing the caravan's early departure. Her *hawdaj* stood waiting outside her tent, while men busily saddled her camel. A sinking feeling washed over her as she realised that her necklace was missing. *Not again*! she thought, scanning her surroundings frantically.

She retraced her steps and remembered that she may have dropped it behind the distant dune where the ladies had been earlier to answer the call of nature. Not wanting to make a scene, she decided to venture out and look for it.

It won't take long, she convinced herself. *It must be over there. It can't be anywhere else*!

As she edged over the sand dune, clutching her outer garment, the encampment vanished from view. Twice she paced the area, eyes scanning the sands, desperately looking for the necklace. Suddenly, a glimmer caught her eye and there she saw the shiny black beads, barely visible under the sand. *Alhamdulillah*! Her search was over.

Aisha hastened back, hitching up her *jilbab* to quicken her steps towards the camp. But as she edged back over the sand dune to rejoin the caravan, her heart sank.

No encampment, no *hawdaj*, and not a single soul in sight. They had disappeared without a trace.

For a moment she was paralysed in breathless disbelief. She was utterly lost, surrounded by endless, undulating dunes. Surely, the men must have assumed that she was in the *hawdaj* since she was so light. They wouldn't realise she was missing until their next stop.

All around her, the vast desert stretched mercilessly under a heavy, overcast sky. Towering sand dunes, shaped by relentless winds, rose and fell in infinite patterns, creating a

maze of golden waves. Aisha wrapped herself tightly in the folds of her *jilbab*. Once tender and golden, the sands now burned fiercely, radiating the sun's merciless heat. Tired by it all, she decided to lie down.

"They will surely realise I'm missing, and come back for me," Aisha whispered to herself amidst the haunting silence of the desert. But for now, in the endless abyss surrounding her, all she could do was place her trust in Allah and wait.

CHAPTER 19
Stranded

"La hawla wa la quwwata illa billah!" At the sound of a man's voice, Aisha's eyes snapped open. Fading dreams scattered into the desert air as she turned her heavy head, trying to shake off the remnants of sleep. She grasped her *jilbab* tightly to cover her face, then blinked hard, struggling to see through the haze as she sat upright.

Peering through the opening of her veil, her eyes looked for signs of life. Just a few feet away stood a young man with his camel. She could be mistaken, but she recognised him as Safwan bin Mu'attal, a loyal Companion of the Prophet ﷺ and a valiant soldier.

Safwan bin Mu'attal had been given a specific duty by the Prophet ﷺ: to stay behind the army and check for any belongings or people left stranded in the rush. He had just arrived at the site of the encampment at dawn when he noticed what looked like a bundle of cloth among the dunes. Curious, he approached to investigate, and to his utter amazement, it was a young lady, lying fast asleep, wrapped in her *jilbab* with only her face uncovered. He recognised her as none other than the Mother of the Believers, Aisha, as he had seen her before the verses of hijab were revealed.

Aisha shuddered, overcome by embarrassment, and didn't utter a word. Sensing her discomfort, Safwan decided not to prolong her torment. Instead, he gestured towards his camel. Bringing the animal down to a seated position, he turned his back to allow Aisha to climb upon it and take her place. Once she was settled, he commanded the camel to rise.

Though weary and parched, Aisha felt a wave of relief wash over her. She was glad to have been found. She sat on the camel's saddle, her mind in a daze, scarcely aware of anything beyond the sound of sand crunching beneath the camel's hooves and the slight friction of the saddle against her leg. Safwan, the respectful young man, walked patiently ahead, holding the camel's reins, as they embarked on the long trek towards the caravan's final stop.

The Prophet ﷺ and his Companions had set up camp at their final station before Madinah, anticipating their entry into the city the next day. That night, verses from Surah Munafiqun were revealed, exposing the deceit of Ibn Salul and the Hypocrites:

"When the Hypocrites come to you, they say,
'We bear witness that you are certainly the Messenger of Allah' – and surely Allah knows that you are His Messenger – but Allah bears witness that the Hypocrites are truly liars... They say,

'If we return to al-Madinah, the mightier ones will surely expel the inferior ones.' But might belongs to Allah and His Messenger, and the Believers, but the Hypocrites do not know."
(Quran, 63:1 & 63:8)

News of the verses unmasking the Hypocrites' true intentions quickly reached the Companions. Everyone felt relieved, expecting an end to the problems caused by the Hypocrites.

Sometime later, a solitary figure with his face wrapped with the end of his turban came galloping towards the encampment. It was Abdullah, the son of Ibn Salul. He had learned of his father's treacherous deeds and the verses of Quran condemning him and the other Hypocrites. Abdullah, who was a true Believer, earnestly approached the Prophet ﷺ to speak to him.

"O Messenger of Allah," he began, his eyes filled with worry. "I have heard about calls to execute my father, Ibn Salul, for his deeds. If it is to be done, then command me to carry out the execution. I fear that if you order someone else to do it, I will not be able to bear seeing the killer of my father alive."

Abdullah's loyalty touched the Prophet ﷺ, but he forbade Abdullah from harbouring ill will towards his father. "No," he said, "deal with him kindly and show him respect while he is among us."

The Quranic verses revealed and unmasked Ibn Salul's true nature, exposing and disgracing him. He realised that the people of Madinah would now despise him, and he could no longer boast to his followers, who had already begun to distance themselves from him. His dream of becoming king of Madinah was shattered forever.

"He humiliates me!" Ibn Salul hissed, his venomous voice dripping with bitterness. All alone in his tent, he realised not even his own sons would stand by him.

"Watch out, Muhammad!" he muttered through clenched teeth. "For the fires of vengeance do burn fiercely within me!" With those words, Ibn Salul feigned a sullen demeanour, casting his eyes downward and clutching his hands to his chest, as if tormented by the cunning of his own machinations.

He stepped out of his tent to find a single ally still by his side. "Who is it that Muhammad loves the most in this world?" Ibn Salul asked.

"Why, someone asked him that very question the other day!" the man replied. Ibn Salul's ears cocked up.

"And?"

"Well, he said, without hesitation, Aisha."

"Aisha?"

"Yes, his wife, Aisha. The man further asked him what about amongst the men..."

"And? What did he say?"

"Her father."

"*Her* father?"

The man nodded, while Ibn Salul became lost in thought. The two men's eyes met, before shifting to two distant figures they spied on the horizon. One was a man, leading the way on foot, while another was seated upon a camel. As the two figures neared the camp, Ibn Salul realised the identity of the lady on the camel. Meeting his friend's gaze, a sly grin spread across his face. "This is going to be too easy!" he declared, marvelling at his own ingenuity. "Time to set the rumour mill in motion!"

CHAPTER 20
The Rumour Mill

"Have you heard?" Ibn Salul murmured, leaning closer to a group of men standing in the shadows of a moonlit alley.

The men could hardly make out who the mysterious figure was, but he had piqued their interest. One man, with a prominent scar across his cheek, raised an eyebrow. "Which news do you refer to?"

"There's talk," Ibn Salul began with a dramatic pause, his gaze sweeping across each face, "of something so unspeakable and unimaginably shameful. I cannot believe she would do such a wicked thing!"

"She?" asked the men in unison. "And who might she be?"

The odious Ibn Salul leaned forward and whispered her name into the ear of one of the men. This man was older, with a grizzly beard, and when he heard her name, his eyes almost popped out of their sockets to Ibn Salul's great satisfaction.

Ibn Salul paused, letting the lie simmer. His drawn brows and solemn expression were pure theatre; beneath it, a smirk of delight flickered briefly across his lips. The thought of his imagined good fortune filled him with quiet glee. This was going to be too easy.

Dusk settled around Umm Ayyub's home. She and her husband Abu Ayyub were from the Ansar and had been Companions of the Prophet ﷺ since they hosted him in their home when he first arrived in Madinah. Umm Ayyub moved through her usual evening rituals, gliding from one lamp to the next, gently extinguishing each flame and surrendering it to the night. Today she was unusually subdued, her lips pressed tightly together, her eyes lost in a labyrinth of thought. Abu Ayyub raised a quizzical brow, noting his wife's change in demeanour.

"What is the matter?" he asked. "Why is there this strange silence lingering in the air?"

Umm Ayyub looked around, surveying the room as though the walls might suddenly sprout ears. When she was convinced it was safe to speak, she could conceal her thoughts no longer.

"O Abu Ayyub," she began, her face creased with worry, "Have you heard what the people are saying about dear Aisha?"

A shadow of recognition crossed Abu Ayyub's eyes. The rumour had reached him, as it had every household in Madinah. Umm Ayyub felt lost in her thoughts, unsure of what to think.

Abu Ayyub's eyes bore deeply into hers, flashing with a mix of anger and unwavering conviction. "Yes, I have indeed heard," he responded, "and these tales are slanderous lies! They are illusions woven by wicked tongues!"

Umm Ayyub's gaze fell, her spirit heavy with shame for even daring to broach the subject. Abu Ayyub stepped closer, tilting Umm Ayyub's chin gently to meet her eyes. "Tell me, O Umm Ayyub," he asked, his tone resolute. "Would you ever do such a thing as they speak of?"

"No, by Allah, I would not dream of it." Umm Ayyub replied, turning away and pressing her hand to her cheek in disgust.

"Know then, that by Allah, Aisha's character shines even brighter than yours!" Abu Ayyub proclaimed.

Umm Ayyub bowed her head, nodding in recognition. Her heart was beating with a symphony of unspoken emotions at the injustice of it all. She silently committed herself to defending Aisha against the vicious tongues that had connived to sully her honour and hurt the Messenger of Allah ﷺ.

CHAPTER 21
Fever Pitch

Aisha had a horrendous fever. The journey had taken its toll on her and now that she was back in her little house in Madinah, she was well and truly bed-bound.

The Messenger of Allah ﷺ felt sorry for her and whenever he entered the room he'd perch at the end of her bed and ask, "How is the lady doing?" But there was something wrong. Aisha noted the merest trace of despondence in his manner, as he didn't seem to be as affectionate towards her as he usually was.

A month went by, and Aisha had all but recovered from her fever when she went out for a walk with her aunt, Umm Mistah. As they returned home, chatting together jovially,

Umm Mistah tripped on the hem of her dress and almost hurtled to the ground.

"Let Mistah be ruined!" she blurted out, to Aisha's horror. It was not like Umm Mistah to curse so easily.

"What a terrible thing you have said," Aisha protested, her eyes blinking in disbelief. "Why would you curse a man who gallantly fought in the Great Battle of Badr?"

"Oh, you *little dear*!" Umm Mistah tutted pityingly. "Have you not heard what he has been saying?"

"No," Aisha replied, genuinely puzzled. "Tell me, what has he been saying?"

Aisha's fever took a turn for the worse. Her head throbbed and her body alternately shivered with cold, then burned hot as a furnace.

"Please," she asked the Messenger of Allah ﷺ, her face expressionless, eyes dim. "May I go to my parents' house?" The Prophet ﷺ agreed at once.

No sooner had she arrived at her parents' house than Aisha threw herself into her mother's arms and sobbed. "O Mother," she whimpered, her face wet with tears, "what are the people saying?"

Umm Ruman bit her lip, her eyes blinking away tears. She turned towards Aisha and stroked her cheek gently. "Sweetheart," she said, "do not let it trouble you. For by Allah, there is rarely a woman out there, of grace and charm, who is adored by her husband, while he has other wives, except that tongues will wag without cause."

Upon hearing this, Aisha cried even more bitterly, her choked sobs and red-rimmed eyes revealing the depth of her pain. "*Subhanallah*!" she whimpered in disbelief. "Are the people really talking in this way?"

She wept and wept as though her heart would burst. All night she cried, tossing and turning, her once youthful cheeks stained with anguish. She simply couldn't sleep.

Zaynab bint Jahsh could hardly believe her ears. Although she'd always been rivals with Aisha, at times competing with her for the Prophet's ﷺ love and attention, she could not believe the people had stooped so low. "I know nothing but virtue in Aisha," Zaynab declared to the Prophet ﷺ, feeling fiercely protective over her co-wife.

Ali sat beside the Messenger of Allah ﷺ, scanning his cousin's downcast eyes. The atmosphere in the small room was tense. They sat in silence for a long while, none of them knowing quite what to say. The Prophet ﷺ looked directly at Ali. "Some day, a matter will arise between you and Aisha," he said. Ali glanced at the curtain behind which Aisha would usually be.

His eyes widened with alarm. "If that day comes, I will be the most wretched of us!" Ali exclaimed.

"No," said the Prophet ﷺ, "but when it happens, return her to her place of safety."

Usama broke in, his voice full of feeling.

"By Allah, we know she is innocent!" he protested, the whiteness of his eyes flashing in contrast to his earthy brown skin.

No revelation had yet come from Allah, and the Prophet ﷺ was deeply troubled by the slanderous rumours swirling around his beloved wife. Unsure how best to respond, he turned to two people especially close to his heart - Ali, whom he had brought up, and Usama, who was like a grandson to him - for counsel.

Ali, seeing his dear cousin looking downcast, spoke gently to reassure him. "O Messenger of Allah ﷺ, Allah has not placed you in a difficult situation, and there are other women you could marry if you wish," he said. "I suggest you ask her maidservant, as she will tell you the truth."

Barirah, Aisha's maidservant, was always by her side and could bear witness to her character. The Prophet ﷺ agreed that if Barirah could vouch for Aisha, he could perhaps put an end to the baseless rumours. So, Allah's Messenger ﷺ called Barirah, and no sooner had he broached the subject, than Barirah began to tell all.

"By Allah, who has sent you with the truth, I have never seen anything blameworthy in Aisha," Barirah began, shrugging her shoulders. "Except - that she is a young girl who sometimes dozes off carelessly, leaving the bread dough out in the open for the goats to gobble up!"

At this they could but smile, though their hearts were heavy with sadness at the slander of Aisha.

CHAPTER 22
Aisha the Pure

The Prophet ﷺ climbed up the pulpit and turned around. The congregation fell silent, the air thick with trepidation. All eyes were on the Messenger of Allah ﷺ.

"O Muslims!" the Prophet ﷺ began. "Who will stand by me in dealing with a man who has hurt me regarding my wife?"

Dozens of eyes shifted towards members of the Khazraj tribe. Everyone knew that Ibn Salul, the instigator of the baseless slander that had hurt the Messenger of Allah ﷺ and his family, was from the Khazraj. A heaviness cloaked the masjid as the Companions' anger grew at the injury suffered by the Messenger of Allah ﷺ and his family.

"By Allah, I have known only goodness in my wife," the Prophet ﷺ continued, his usually bright eyes dimmed with sorrow. "Yet they accuse a man of wrongdoing, about whom I know only good. He has never entered my house except in my company."

The man the Prophet ﷺ spoke of was, of course, Safwan, who was being cruelly slandered because of his chivalry.

The chief of the Aws tribe stood up abruptly, upset that it had come to this. "O Messenger of Allah!" he said, his voice clear with conviction. "Grant me the honour of addressing this matter. If he is of the Aws tribe, my hand seals his fate. But if he is of our brethren, the Khazraj, then command us and we shall fulfil your command."

At this, the leader of the Khazraj tribe leapt to his feet, the fires of tribal honour burning in his heart. "By Allah, you have told a lie! You shall not and cannot kill anyone from our tribe. Would you be singing the same tune if the man was from your tribe, Aws?"

Emotions surged, threatening the serenity of the masjid.

"By Allah!" a man from Aws called out. "It is you who are the liar! If you won't kill him, we surely will! For you are a hypocrite, defending the Hypocrites!"

For a moment, the masjid teetered on the brink of chaos, and they almost forgot that their brotherhood as Muslims overrode the tribalism of the Age of Ignorance. But the Prophet ﷺ, with his commanding presence and wise words, quelled the rising storm and brought them back to their senses.

Once they had calmed down, they felt ashamed of their tribalistic wrangling and a hush fell over the crowd.

Meanwhile, Aisha's tears knew no end. The sparkle had dimmed in her eyes, for she had wept continuously for two nights. The sole glimmer of solace that comforted her, was knowing Zaynab had defended her.

"Allah protected her from speaking ill of me. It is a testament to her deep devotion to Him," Aisha remarked, with a soft glow in her eyes.

That day, an Ansari woman came to visit Aisha at her parents' house. No sooner had Aisha allowed her in than they sat, clasped hands and shed silent tears. Not a word was exchanged, and not a word was required. Aisha was deeply touched that the lady had come as a sister in Islam to share in her pain. While they wept, Aisha's parents welcomed Allah's Messenger ﷺ. He came and sat down near Aisha. No revelation had come to the Prophet ﷺ for a month. Aisha's grief weighed so heavily that she couldn't even lift her eyes to meet his.

The Prophet ﷺ recited a prayer and then said gently, "O Aisha, some things have reached me about you, so if you are innocent, Allah will soon bring your innocence to light.

But if you made a mistake, then repent and seek Allah's forgiveness, for when a person admits his sin and asks Allah for forgiveness, Allah accepts his repentance."

Rasulullah ﷺ cared deeply about Aisha and knew she was a servant of Allah before she was his wife. He didn't have knowledge of the unseen. He only wanted to guide her and only wanted good for her.

Aisha's tears dried up all of a sudden. She shot a glance towards her father, pleading with him to say something.

"Respond to Allah's Messenger!" she said.

"By Allah, I do not know what to say to Allah's Messenger." Abu Bakr replied.

Aisha turned to her mother in anguish. "Talk to Allah's Messenger on my behalf," she pleaded.

Umm Ruman shook her head, her eyes cast downward. "By Allah, I do not know what to say to Allah's Messenger," she replied.

"By Allah," Aisha cried, "I know you have heard this slander so many times that it has no doubt taken root in your hearts and you have taken it as the truth. Now, if I tell you I *am* innocent, and Allah knows I am innocent, you will not believe me! And if I falsely confess to you about it, and Allah knows I am innocent, you will surely believe me."

Her parents sat speechless, looking down at the ground.

"By Allah, the only comparison I can make between you and me is to the father of Prophet Yusuf when he said, *'Fa sabrun jameel'*. So, patience is the most beautiful response.

And it is Allah I turn to for help regarding what you are saying."

With that, Aisha turned away from them, her gaze fixed on the wall where she lay. She prayed that Allah would intervene, perhaps by sending a dream to the Prophet ﷺ to confirm her innocence.

CHAPTER 23
Divine Intervention

It was a chilling winter's day when the Prophet ﷺ had come to visit Aisha at her father's house. There, in the midst of their gathering, an extraordinary event unfolded. The Prophet ﷺ, overtaken by a divine force, began to sweat profusely. Despite the cold, his brow glistened with droplets that fell like precious diamonds. Those present looked on, awestruck, as Quranic verses were revealed before their eyes:

"It was a group from among you that concocted the lie - do not consider it a bad thing for you; it was a good thing - and every one of them will be charged with the sin he has earned.

He who took the greatest part in it will have a painful punishment.When you heard the lie, why did the believing men and women not think well of their own people and declare, 'This is obviously a lie'? And why did the accusers not bring four witnesses to it? If they cannot produce such witnesses, they are the liars in Allah's eyes. If it were not for Allah's bounty and mercy towards you in this world and the next, you would already have been afflicted by terrible suffering for indulging in such talk. When you took it up with your tongues, and spoke with your mouths things you did not know to be true, you thought it was trivial, but to Allah it was grave. When you heard the lie, why did you not say, 'We should not repeat this – Allah forbid – It is a monstrous slander'? Allah warns you never to do anything like this again, if you are true Believers. Allah makes His messages clear to you: Allah is All-Knowing, All-Wise..."

(Quran, 24:11-18)

After the divine verses were delivered, the force that overtook the Messenger of Allah ﷺ released its grip. With a radiant smile, he looked at Aisha and declared, "Aisha! Praise be to Allah! Your innocence has been affirmed."

Umm Ruman's eyes brightened and her tense shoulders relaxed. "Go to Allah's Messenger!" she urged Aisha with a prod.

"By Allah, I will not go to him and will not thank anyone but Allah!" Aisha replied emphatically, falling onto her face in prostration.

Tears glistened in Aisha's eyes and warmth flooded her cheeks. "I had merely hoped that Allah's Messenger ﷺ might have a dream in which Allah would prove my innocence," she said. "By Allah, I never imagined that Allah would reveal divine revelation about me, as I considered myself too insignificant to be spoken of in the Quran!"

Abu Bakr was still upset to see how much anguish his daughter had endured. "By Allah," he vowed. "I will never provide Mistah with anything after what he said about Aisha." Everyone knew that Abu Bakr had always been generous, caring for his cousin's son, Mistah, by sending him money for his needs. Yet, Mistah was among those who had spread the rumour.

But Allah revealed verses encouraging Abu Bakr and the Muslims to forgive and continue being charitable to their relatives, despite any harm they might have endured:

"Those of you who have been graced with plenty
should not swear that they will no longer give to relatives,
the poor and those who emigrate in Allah's way: let them pardon
and forgive. Do you not wish for Allah to forgive you?
Allah is Most Forgiving, Most Merciful."
(Quran, 24:22)

For those who were guilty of slandering Aisha, the punishment was 80 lashes, a reminder of the severity of their crime.

Upon hearing Allah's divine command, Abu Bakr's heart softened. "Yes, by Allah! I do wish for Allah to forgive me," and so he continued to support and help Mistah as he had always done.

CHAPTER 24
Ibn Salul Meets His Maker

There was a funeral taking place, and Aisha could hear the people gathering in the masjid, speaking in whispers. It was true. Ibn Salul, the chief of the Hypocrites, was dead.

Although she had not been at the grave site herself, the news of what occurred had quickly reached Aisha's ears, painting a vivid picture in her mind. Abdullah, the son of Ibn Salul, had stood weeping over his father's grave. The image of his grief touched Aisha's heart, despite his father's complex legacy.

Ibn Salul had been a source of great distress for Aisha, especially during the time of the slander. She remembered the hurtful rumours Ibn Salul had spread, casting doubt on her reputation - a trial that had deeply wounded her and strained the community. The echoes of that pain were still present in her heart, making the news of his burial a moment of mixed emotions.

As the burial of Ibn Salul was about to take place, Abdullah's anguish became unbearable. The anguish his father had caused the family of Rasulullah ﷺ was unforgivable. And yet, he was still his father and his heart still ached for him.

Gripped by the thought of the punishment his father was about to face in the grave, Abdullah urgently sought a way to alleviate his doom. In a desperate plea, Abdullah implored the Prophet ﷺ, "O Allah's Messenger! Please drape my father in your shirt, one that has touched your skin."

The Messenger of Allah ﷺ saw the sadness in Abdullah's eyes and comforted him. He understood that pain all too well - the pain of loving someone deeply, yet not being able to guide their heart to faith. Years ago, he had stood by the deathbed of Abu Talib, the uncle who had raised him like a father, shielding him when no one else would. The sorrow of losing him had been heavy - not only because of the bond they shared, but because Abu Talib had left this world without uttering the words that would have saved him.

He had also parted with Khadijah, his most loyal Companion. And over time, he had buried his beloved daughters - first Ruqayyah, then Zainab, and most recently Umm Kulthum.

Now, with quiet strength and serenity, the Prophet ﷺ approached Ibn Salul's grave. The crowd, in silent anticipation, watched closely. He signalled to have Ibn Salul's body lifted up with a gentle motion.

The air was thick with unspoken questions as the Prophet ﷺ stood by the grave. He leaned forward and gently blew over the body - a quiet gesture of compassion, for even those who had wronged him. Then, with tenderness and honour for Abdullah, his devoted Companion and the grieving son, the Prophet ﷺ removed his own shirt and draped it over Ibn Salul. The crowd watched, spellbound by the gravity of the gesture.

The Prophet ﷺ got up to offer the funeral prayer when the voice of Umar cut through the quiet. "O Allah's Messenger!" he said, holding on to the Prophet's ﷺ robe. "Will you really offer the funeral prayer for Ibn Salul, after he said what he said and after the strife he caused?" Umar's voice faltered in sheer incredulity.

"Leave me be, O Umar," the Prophet ﷺ responded, for he wanted nothing more than to see people saved from the Hellfire. "I have been given the choice and I have chosen to do it. If I knew that seeking Allah's forgiveness for him more than 70 times would grant him forgiveness, I would have done so."

Not long after the funeral, Allah revealed verses of the Quran correcting the Prophet ﷺ and instructing him never to pray over any of the Hypocrites again. Once more, the revelation had concurred with the intuition of Umar. This command came from Allah because the Hypocrites had their chance in life but chose to keep denying Allah and His Messenger ﷺ. They plotted against the Believers, allying with their enemies to harm them. Even in their final moments, they were stubborn in their disbelief, filled with hatred and evil schemes against Allah and His Messenger ﷺ. Allah revealed in the Quran:

> *"And never offer a prayer upon any one of them who dies, and do not stand by his grave. They disbelieved in Allah and His Messenger and died while they were sinners."*
> (Quran, 9:84)

Nine long years after the Hijrah, Ibn Salul was gone. Time finally extinguished his once formidable influence. *How swiftly fortunes had turned*, Aisha thought. Why, it was only yesterday that she had moved into her little home, heart full of wonder and hope. But so much had changed since then.

Among the hardest of those changes was the loss of her beloved mother. Umm Ruman - the gentle, steadfast woman who had nourished and raised her, who had stood by her through the storm of the slander - had now returned to Allah. Aisha missed her every day. But even in that sadness, there was a glimmer of comfort: her brother Abdurrahman had finally accepted Islam, something Umm Ruman had long hoped for.

Abdurrahman had once stood on the opposite side of the battlefield, fighting against the Muslims with a hardened heart. He had clung stubbornly to the ways of his tribe, refusing to believe. But now, he had joined the Believers, his heart softened by the truth, and his loyalty redirected to Allah and His Messenger ﷺ.

Soon afterwards the Muslims liberated Makkah, freeing the Ka'bah from false idols and returning it to the worship of Allah alone. After the great Conquest of Makkah, the light of Islam swiftly swept across Arabia, reaching every dwelling, from the humblest tents to the grandest forts.

Old foes, such as Abu Jahl, had either been defeated or, like Abu Sufyan, embraced the Prophet's ﷺ message. Meanwhile, the murmurs of the Hypocrites in Madinah faded into oblivion. Their menacing influence became a distant memory, as people flocked to embrace the clear and irresistible truth of the Prophet's ﷺ call.

Abu Bakr was greatly pleased. Both his father, Abu Quhafah, and his son, Abdurrahman, had now entered Islam. One day, Abdurrahman recalled in front of him that during the Battle of Badr, while still a Disbeliever, he had the chance to kill his father but turned away to avoid him. Upon hearing this, Abu Bakr raised his brow at his son and retorted, "If I had encountered you that day, I would not have spared you!" And he meant it.

As for Aisha's grandfather, Abu Quhafah, it was during the Conquest of Makkah, when the Muslims entered the city victorious, and the Prophet ﷺ made his way to the Ka'bah, that Abu Bakr brought the elderly man to meet him. Abu Quhafah's hair was even whiter with age and his body frail. Abu Bakr gently led him forward, but when the Prophet ﷺ saw him he expressed concern, saying, "Why did you not leave the *shaykh* in his house so that I could come to him?"

"O Messenger of Allah," Abu Bakr replied, "it is more fitting for him to walk to you than for you to walk to him."

With that, Abu Quhafah was seated before the Prophet ﷺ, who placed his hand on the old man's chest and said softly, "Embrace Islam, and you will find peace". The kindness of the Prophet ﷺ and the truth of his words filled Abu Quhafah's heart, leading him to accept Islam.

"Ash-hadu an la ilaha illallah, wa ash-hadu anna Muhammadur Rasulullah!"

"I bear witness," Abu Quhafah had said, like so many before him and so many who would come after him, "that there is nothing worthy of worship except Allah, and I bear witness that Muhammad is the Messenger of Allah."

After the Conquest of Makkah, the Prophet's ﷺ mission was complete. It was then that Surah an-Nasr was revealed:

"In the Name of Allah, Most Gracious, Most Merciful
When Allah's help and victory come. And you (O Prophet)
see people entering Allah's religion in crowds. Then glorify
the praises of your Lord and seek His forgiveness.
Surely He is Ever-Accepting of Repentance."
(Quran, 110)

CHAPTER 25
In Aisha's Arms

Heart racing, Aisha awakened from her dream, its imagery still clear and haunting. When her father came by the house that day, she was bursting to tell him about her vision. "Dear Father!" she exclaimed. "I saw in a dream, not one, but three moons fall into my room!"

"*Subhanallah!*" Abu Bakr remarked, his gaze distant as he pondered the dream's meaning. "If this was a truthful dream, then it could be that these walls are destined to house the souls of the three most auspicious people on Earth." Aisha rubbed her forehead in bewilderment, puzzled by this interpretation.

The sun was high when the Prophet ﷺ returned from the Baqi cemetery after attending a funeral. His body ached and every step felt laboured. As he entered, he heard Aisha's groans. She was lying in bed, her hands clutching her temples. Their gazes met for a moment.

"Such an ache..." Aisha murmured.

"My pain mirrors yours," the Prophet ﷺ said, feeling his head throb. Then with a glint of humour in his eyes, he said, "Why worry, O Aisha? Should you pass away before me, my love, rest assured I would oversee your farewell fittingly."

Aisha shot him a playful smile. "I'm sure you would, and perhaps you would introduce a new wife into my house?"

But as the days rolled on, the levity faded. The Prophet's ﷺ strength waned, and every task became more and more difficult.

Despite his illness, the Prophet ﷺ continued to lead prayers. Until one day, as he was in the masjid, his legs gave way and he fell to the ground. Two men came to his aid, his arms draped around their necks as they carefully carried him back to Aisha's home, his legs barely skimming the ground.

After the near-collapse in the masjid, it was evident to all, especially to the wives of the Prophet ﷺ, that the situation was dire. They all agreed to allow the Prophet ﷺ to stay in Aisha's house, for they knew it was where he found the most comfort.

When he heard the next call to prayer echo from the masjid, the Prophet ﷺ turned to Aisha. His voice was weak when he asked, "Have the prayers begun?"

"They have not, O Messenger of Allah," Aisha replied softly, "for the people await you."

The Prophet ﷺ used all of the effort he could muster to push himself up. "Prepare water," he said, "so that I may make *wudu*."

He washed his hands, face and arms, performing the *wudu*. But just as he was about to reach the door, he fell unconscious onto the floor.

Aisha screamed and rushed to help him, pulling his head and shoulders onto her lap. Her soft prayers filled the room as she willed him back.

Upon regaining consciousness, the Prophet's ﷺ gaze found hers. "Did they perform the prayer?" he whispered.

She shook her head. "No, O Messenger of Allah, they are waiting for you."

With great effort, the Prophet ﷺ gestured to her and spoke. "Tell Abu Bakr to lead them."

Aisha hesitated. "But Messenger of Allah, my father's heart is tender, he cannot hold back tears when reciting the Quran. Why not assign someone else?"

But the Prophet's ﷺ command was final. "Abu Bakr must lead!" he insisted. So, they sent for Abu Bakr, who began leading the Muslims in prayer.

One day, as Abu Bakr's voice resonated in the masjid, the Prophet ﷺ experienced a brief improvement in his health. Aided by two Companions, he made a frail appearance during one of the prayers. When Abu Bakr sensed his presence, he tried to step aside to allow the Prophet ﷺ to lead the prayer. But a gentle gesture from the Prophet ﷺ signalled him to remain in place. The Prophet ﷺ then sat down beside Abu Bakr, who continued to lead the prayer.

Aisha remembered how, during earlier illnesses, the Prophet ﷺ would recite *surahs* and blow his blessed breath over his body for healing and protection. But now he lacked the strength to do even that.

Sensing this, Aisha began reciting Surah al-Falaq and Surah an-Nas onto the Prophet's ﷺ blessed hands and rubbing them over his body, hoping for their blessings. Aisha served the Prophet ﷺ in every way she could. She fetched water for him, helped him make *wudu*, fed him, and combed his hair and beard. So devoted was she, that she learned many homemade remedies suggested by well-wishers and visitors, and tried various potions and medicines to treat the Prophet's ﷺ symptoms.

Despite his suffering, the Messenger of Allah ﷺ was determined to settle all his worldly matters. One morning, he asked, "O Aisha, what have you done with the pieces of gold we had?"

"I've kept them," she replied.

"Distribute them to the needy," the Prophet ﷺ instructed. When she hesitated to do so, he urged her again. As she handed the gold to him, the Prophet ﷺ remarked, "How can Muhammad meet his Creator while clinging to these?"

Without delay, he ﷺ gave them away in charity.

The Prophet ﷺ signalled for the curtain of Aisha's *hujrah*, which opened into the masjid, to be drawn aside. Though weakened by illness, he managed to stand by the door, watching his devoted followers as they prayed.

A familiar and reassuring voice echoed from the masjid: *"Allahu Akbar!"* It was Abu Bakr leading the prayer. As the prayer began, Rasulullah ﷺ found the strength to shuffle closer, his gaze capturing the sight of the Believers united, praying shoulder to shoulder. A smile spread across his face and immense pride for his Ummah swelled within his heart. These were the very souls he had nurtured, guiding them through tribulations and triumphs alike. Together, they had faced life's tests, celebrated victories and mourned losses.

Emerging from the oppressive shadows of Makkah, the Muslims now illuminated Arabia with the light of Islam.

As he watched his Companions praying that day, a surge of energy coursed through him, urging him to his feet one more time. The people sensed his presence as he leaned against the door frame, signalling for them to continue, his face radiating approval.

Today, he stood mightier than both Caesar and the Pope, despite lacking a palace or bodyguards. His true strength lay in the Message of Allah he bore and the devoted Companions by his side. With unshakeable faith, he knew Allah had destined that even when he was gone, Islam's message would reach every home.

CHAPTER 26
The Pain of Goodbye

"*La ilaha illallah!*" the Prophet ﷺ said in a hoarse whisper, his breath heavy, his forehead dripping with sweat. "Truly, death has its agonies!"

Aisha cradled his ailing body in her lap, trying to offer solace. Her fingers weaved through his beard, moving her position to make him comfortable.

The door creaked open to reveal Fatima, her eyes filled with tears at the sight of her ailing father.

"O my father!" Fatima cried, seeing the Prophet ﷺ wince with pain. "What great pain my father is in!"

"Your father will suffer no more after today," the Prophet ﷺ whispered. He reached for a basin of water, wetting his hand and wiping his face. "O Allah, give me the strength to face the pains of death," he murmured. Aisha held him, her eyes filled with melancholy, as she silently prayed.

Then the Prophet ﷺ managed to sit up and gestured for Fatima to sit next to him. The Prophet ﷺ tenderly whispered something into her ear. She began to weep even more profusely. Seeing this, he whispered something else into her ear and her tears ceased. Her eyes glistened as she smiled and even let out a laugh.

Before Fatima departed, Aisha stopped her for a moment in the courtyard. Fatima bore a striking resemblance to her father, reflecting his features and mannerisms in her every movement.

"I never saw joy so close to sadness like I saw today," Aisha remarked curiously. "What did the Prophet ﷺ share with you, O Fatima?"

Fatima seemed unsure for a moment. "I'm not one to disclose the secret of the Messenger of Allah," she said firmly, wanting to honour the trust of the Prophet ﷺ.

Once Fatima had left, Aisha's brother, Abdurrahman, stepped in, the concern palpable in his eyes. By now, the Prophet ﷺ could barely muster the strength to speak. As Aisha tried to gauge the Prophet's ﷺ condition, she noticed him looking at the *miswak* toothbrush in her brother's hand.

"Would you like me to bring it to you?" Aisha asked tenderly. The Prophet ﷺ nodded in response. "Shall I soften it for you?" she inquired again, and once more, he nodded.

Taking the *miswak*, she chewed on it to soften its end and rubbed it on his teeth. But as she did so, the Prophet ﷺ momentarily lost consciousness, causing Aisha to hold him tighter, tears streaming down. She could hear his heart pounding and his forehead was a furnace. She dabbed the Prophet's ﷺ brow with a cooling wet cloth.

When the Prophet ﷺ regained his senses, he stared at the ceiling, seemingly listening, and then said with surprising clarity, "O Allah... I choose the Highest Companion."

A memory flashed through Aisha's mind: the Prophet ﷺ once mentioned Prophets are given a choice before they pass away. It seemed he had made his. Aisha began to sob. "He is not choosing us!" With her eyes closed and her arms cradling his head, she held him against her bosom. Moments later, she felt the weight of his departure.

He had gone.

In the stillness that enveloped her, she tried to grasp the depth of her loss.

He was gone.

How lonely the world would be without Rasulullah ﷺ! How fortunate they had been to turn to him for every question and every concern. How easily he had put their hearts at rest!

Outside, the masjid was a tempest of emotion. Umar's voice, raw with denial, boomed with anger. "He is not dead! I'll challenge anyone who dares claim it!" Umar was brandishing his sword, ready to strike.

Across the masjid floor, Abu Bakr cut through the throng. Upon entering Aisha's house, he beheld the heart-wrenching scene: Aisha's scarf wet with grief, Rasulullah ﷺ lying in front of her, his body covered with a cloth.

Tenderly, he uncovered the Prophet's ﷺ serene face. "You shine brightly, in both life and death, O Messenger of Allah," he whispered. "May my father and mother be sacrificed for you. By Allah, you will not taste two deaths. The death that was decreed for you, you have just experienced it."

His emotions swelled as he placed a gentle kiss on his dear friend's forehead one last time. Then, gathering himself, Abu Bakr rose and entered the masjid through Aisha's *hujrah*. With the weight of the entire Ummah on his shoulders and love for the Prophet ﷺ pounding in his chest, Abu Bakr stepped into the unfolding chaos.

"Sit down, O Umar!" Abu Bakr commanded. Umar lowered his sword immediately and a hush fell over the masjid.

With a voice full of comforting authority, Abu Bakr proclaimed: "Whoever used to worship Muhammad ﷺ, know that Muhammad has died. But whoever worships Allah - He is Ever-Living and never dies."

Locking eyes with each stunned face before him, he began to recite Allah's verses:

"Muhammad is no more than a Messenger;
other Messengers have gone before him.
If he were to die or to be killed, would you turn back
on your heels? Those who do so will not harm Allah
whatsoever. And Allah will reward those
who are grateful."
(Quran, 3:144)

Although the Companions knew the verses well, it was as if they were hearing them for the first time on this darkest of dark days. Umar was lost for words and his legs failed him. The masjid was filled with the sorrowful sounds of grief and mourning which rippled throughout Madinah.

The people of Madinah agreed they had never witnessed a brighter day than the one, 11 years earlier, when the Messenger of Allah ﷺ arrived in their city. In stark contrast, they had never known a more sorrowful day than the day he passed away. Aisha did not know how this awful ache she felt in her heart would ever leave her.

Down the alleyway, poor Umm Ayman, the Prophet's ﷺ foster mother, sat on her doorstep with her scarf soaked in tears. When people tried to console her, she said, "I knew well that the Messenger of Allah ﷺ would die one day. I cry not only for his departure; I cry because revelation has now been lifted from us."

And so, they all wept for all they had lost with the passing of Rasulullah ﷺ.

He was the light that shone through darkest night,
The one we sought to lead us ever-right.
The day they placed him in Earth's quiet enclave,
Layered soil upon him, in that silent grave.
Would that Allah took every one of us,
Leaving neither man nor woman, thus.

CHAPTER 27
Daughter of the Caliph

Everyone had an opinion about where the Prophet ﷺ ought to be buried.

"Bury him near his mimbar, the place where he led prayer."

"No, he would want to be buried with his Companions in the Garden of Baqi."

"No, no! That is for us commoners! We must honour him more than that!"

"But he warned us not to make his grave a place of worship."

Abu Bakr listened intently to what the Sahaba were saying.

"I heard the Messenger of Allah ﷺ say that Prophets are always buried in the spot where they die," Abu Bakr said.

They asked Aisha's permission and removed the mattress upon which the Prophet ﷺ had passed away. Aisha could hear the *clunk, clunk* of tools digging the ground in her room.

And so, the Prophet ﷺ was buried in the very spot upon which he passed away, in Aisha's house. People entered her house in shifts, 10 by 10 to pray for him. First, his family members and clansmen from Banu Hashim, then the Muhajirun who had migrated with him from Makkah all those years ago, and then the Ansar, the people of Madinah who had granted him refuge. Then came the women to pray in shifts, followed by the children. It took almost two days for everyone to pay their respects.

Next door, Fatima wept openly when she was told of her father's burial.

"O Fatima, tell us now, what made you smile before the passing of Rasulullah?" Aisha asked. Now that the Prophet ﷺ had passed away, Fatima was ready to speak.

"He told me: 'Every year, Jibreel used to revise the Quran with me once, but this year he has done so twice'." Fatima's cheeks glistened with streaks of tear marks. "He said, 'I think it is nothing but a portent of my death. And you will be the first of my family to follow me'. That's when I started crying.

But then he said, 'Wouldn't you like to be the chief of all the ladies of Paradise?' That's when I laughed."

After the funeral prayers had finished, Aisha continued to live in her home. Her father, Abu Bakr, placed his hand on her shoulder and said, "This was one of your moons, O Aisha," reminding her of the dream she had so many years ago, "and he is the best of them."

The grave was a neat, unmarked space on one side of her room. Once in a while, she'd glance at it, comforted that her beloved was somehow still near.

A meeting of the senior Companions took place and Umar locked eyes with each of the men present. "The Prophet ﷺ chose Abu Bakr to lead the people in prayer during his illness," Umar said. "So, which of us would want to put ourselves forward, ahead of Abu Bakr?" No one did.

The next day, Umar stood up in the masjid of the Prophet ﷺ and announced, "Allah has brought you together and united you under a new leader." He paused to let the gravity of his words sink in.

Thus, the Companions of the Prophet ﷺ nominated Aisha's father to be the caliph and Commander of the Faithful.

"He is the best among you, he is the Companion of the Messenger of Allah ﷺ and was the second of the two when they hid in the cave during the Hijrah, as mentioned in the Quran," Umar said, his voice growing firmer as he spoke. "So, stand up and pledge your allegiance to him."

Abu Bakr looked reluctant, but the Muhajirun and the Ansar lined up in the masjid to place their hands in his.

"Climb the pulpit!" Umar urged Abu Bakr. Hesitantly, Abu Bakr complied.

After praising Allah, the new caliph, Abu Bakr, addressed the people:

"O people, I have been appointed over you, though I am not the best among you. If I act correctly, then help me. And if I act wrongly, then correct me."

He looked over the congregation, his voice steady and resolute.

"The weak among you will be strong in my eyes until their rights have been vindicated, and the strong among you shall be weak in my eyes until I have taken what is due from them. Obey me as long as I obey Allah and His Prophet ﷺ; if I disobey Him and His Prophet, then obey me not." He concluded, "And now, rise for prayers. May Allah have mercy on you!"

It came in waves. First, an aching, overwhelming sense of loss, like the world had frozen. Then a deep yearning that seemed to emanate from within her chest. Aisha wondered when the swirling memories, whirling grief and twirling faces of visitors would subside. Maybe one day she would wake up and this would all just be a dream. The days were long and the nights unbearably lonely, but Aisha found solace in her prayers.

Aisha was comforted in the knowledge the Prophet ﷺ had once told her that Angel Jibreel came to him with a picture of her on a green, silken cloth and said to him: "Indeed, this is your wife in this world and in the Hereafter."

Knowing she would meet him again one fine day, and be his wife in Paradise, gave her immense hope.

Though the Prophet ﷺ was no longer with them, he had not left his followers without guidance. Aisha knew that she, along with the entire Muslim Ummah, would now need to follow the timeless advice he had given during his farewell sermon, when he said: "I have left you with two guides that will never lead you astray, as long as you hold firmly to them: the Book of Allah and the *Sunnah* of His Prophet."

The Book of Allah was the Quran. The Sunnah was the Prophet's ﷺ sayings, actions and example. For he had been the living embodiment of the Quran's teachings.

The wives of the Prophet ﷺ and his daughter, Fatima, were counted from among the relatives known as *Ahl al-Bayt*, 'the people of his household'. They were revered and respected in the community.

Soon after the Prophet ﷺ passed away, they sent Uthman bin Affan to Abu Bakr, seeking clarification about the Prophet's ﷺ inheritance.

However, Aisha, who was deeply knowledgeable about the Prophet's ﷺ teachings, reminded them the Messenger of Allah ﷺ had specifically said about Prophets: "Our property cannot be inherited, and whatever we leave is to be spent in charity."

To honour the Prophet's ﷺ wishes after his death, Abu Bakr ensured the distribution of his wealth as charity. In place of an inheritance, he established a regular income for the *Ahl al-Bayt* which included the Prophet's ﷺ wives and daughters, like Aisha, Hafsah and Fatima. Ali comforted his wife, Fatima, who was still grieving the loss of her father. Abu Bakr reminded her this arrangement was in line with the Prophet's ﷺ wishes and, with time, Fatima understood the decision.

Abu Bakr's time as caliph lasted only two years, but his leadership was crucial for the Ummah. He acted quickly and decisively during the Ridda Wars, when several tribes rebelled and refused to pay the zakah. Zakah, or compulsory charity, is one of the five pillars of Islam, alongside the five daily prayers, fasting in Ramadan, Hajj, and the testimony of faith. These pillars are essential for every Muslim to fulfil, and zakah, in particular, is the duty of the wealthy to support the poor. Abu Bakr understood he had to uphold Allah's laws, just as the Prophet ﷺ had commanded them to do.

Another challenge came from Musaylimah the Liar, who falsely claimed prophethood and attracted a large following. By defeating these rebels, Abu Bakr helped to keep the Ummah united. He also expanded the Islamic lands by launching campaigns against the Byzantine and Persian empires, paving the way for future victories.

One of Abu Bakr's greatest contributions was gathering the Quran into one written book. While many, like Aisha herself, had memorised the Quran, Abu Bakr recognised the importance of having a single, accurate copy of the scripture. By appointing Zayd bin Thabit, the Prophet's ﷺ scribe, to oversee this effort, he ensured that the Quran would be safeguarded for future generations. Even though his reign would be short, his actions set an example of fairness, strength, and commitment to Islam that future caliphs would follow.

It was only a few months into Abu Bakr's Caliphate that the Prophet's ﷺ beloved daughter, Fatima, passed away. It was exactly as the Prophet ﷺ had informed her - she was indeed the first to join him. Her husband, Ali, buried her quietly at night, just as she had wished.

Soon after, Abu Bakr visited Ali. Tears flowed from his eyes as he said, "By Allah, being good to the family of the

Prophet ﷺ is even dearer to me than being good to my own family."

Aisha was very sad. She had lost a relative who was a dear neighbour and friend.

Eventually, the day came that Aisha had been dreading. Abu Bakr was ill and on his deathbed. Aisha sat at his bedside and softly recited poetry in his praise:

"So pure, even rain clouds are quenched by his countenance,
He is the spring breeze for orphans, protector of widows..."

When he heard this, Abu Bakr gazed out of his window. "That describes Rasulullah ﷺ," he said, yearning for his dear friend.

"My daughter, on which day did the Messenger of Allah ﷺ die?"

"On a Monday," she replied.

"What day is it today?"

"It is Monday, my father."

"I feel I too will pass by this evening," Abu Bakr went on. "With what did you shroud the Prophet ﷺ?"

"With three white Yemeni garments."

"Wash this garment and add two more for my shroud, my daughter," Abu Bakr instructed.

"But this sheet is old, father," Aisha protested.

"The living have a greater need for new cloth than the dead!" Abu Bakr replied.

"My darling daughter," Abu Bakr continued, looking agitated, "go and see how much extra wealth I have acquired since becoming caliph and send that amount to whoever is caliph after me."

Abu Bakr then said, "O Aisha, there is no one in my family more beloved to me than you. Nonetheless, you took some fruits from one of my gardens and I feel uncomfortable about it. Will you return the fruits so I can divide them fairly among your two brothers and two sisters?"

"Yes, of course, my father," Aisha replied. "But I only have one sister. Who is my other sister?" Aisha was perplexed since Asma was her only sister, as far as she was aware.

"She is in the womb of my wife, Habibah bint Kharijah," Abu Bakr responded. "It has been cast into my mind that the child is a baby girl, so make sure you look after her."

Aisha wept, seeing her father's state and nodded obediently.

Abu Bakr began breathing heavily. "From the day I was put in charge of the Muslims," he said. "I have not taken a single extra dinar or dirham from them. I have put the least desirable food in my stomach and have put on my back the coarsest of garments. I donate my orchard to charity, to cover the salary that Umar forced me to take as caliph, for my expenses."

When they checked Abu Bakr's wealth, they found the only thing he had gained since becoming caliph was one camel and a servant. Abu Bakr's servant, camel and orchard were entrusted to Umar. They also delivered the copy of the Quran Abu Bakr had compiled to Umar's safekeeping. When Umar saw that Abu Bakr had returned these things, tears began falling down his face and he cried so much, the surrounding ground became wet.

"May Allah have mercy on Abu Bakr," Umar said. "Ever since the Prophet ﷺ died, Abu Bakr has worked himself to exhaustion."

"Let my wife, Asma bint Umais, wash my body for burial," Abu Bakr instructed, "and bury me next to Rasulullah ﷺ."

Then Aisha's father uttered his final words, the words of the Quran:

"Let me die as a Muslim,
and join me with the righteous people."
(Quran, 12:101)

Abu Bakr had been a wealthy merchant. He had shown Aisha the importance of using his wealth to benefit others. Material possessions such as money, houses, gardens and riches were not inherently bad. On the contrary, they were tools for doing good and earning rewards in the afterlife. It was important not to become attached to wealth, but to use it to support those in need and to share the message of Islam, making an impact in the world.

Aisha had grown up in the tender care of her father and then been nurtured in the loving heart of Rasulullah ﷺ. They had been her guides, her supporters and her teachers. As a wife, she knew her role in supporting the Prophet ﷺ in his home. As a daughter of the caliph, Aisha had helped her father, informing him using the knowledge she had whenever he had sought her counsel.

Aisha would never marry again, since it was forbidden to marry the Mothers of the Believers. Who could compare to the Prophet ﷺ as a husband, anyway? She had no children of her own and knew she never would, now that the Prophet ﷺ had passed.

Time would not hold its breath, moving ever swiftly forward like an unstoppable wind. How must she proceed without the presence of the two men who had loved her the most and guided her life so profoundly? In the stillness of her thoughts, she pondered what path Allah was asking her to take now. What purpose awaited her in this new chapter of life?

Aisha knew only Prophets received direct revelation, yet she understood Believers could still find inspiration and guidance from Allah if they listened closely. She prayed Allah would guide her in her quest to uncover how she could best serve Him.

CHAPTER 28
Hajj at Last

Many of the Companions of the Prophet ﷺ had by now left Madinah and travelled far and wide to spread the message of Islam, to protect the borders of the Muslim lands, and to teach the new Muslims how to worship Allah. It was a time of great change.

Umar was chosen as the next caliph, and during his reign, the Muslims conquered Shaam to the northwest, Iraq to the northeast, and Egypt to the west. In each new land, they established provinces with new governors. In Shaam, Umar appointed Mu'awiyah, the son of Abu Sufyan as governor. Egypt's new governor was the Companion of the Prophet ﷺ, Amr bin al-Aas, who established a capital city, Fustat, near the banks of the Nile, and the first masjid in Africa.

Iraq's governor was the Companion Abu Musa al-Ash'ari, who was also a great teacher and scholar.

One day, Abu Musa al-Ash'ari was sitting with a congregation in Iraq, discussing matters of religion and narrating sayings of the Prophet ﷺ to his students. People would come from far and wide to Basra or Kufa, Iraq's largest cities, to seek knowledge from the great Abu Musa.

"Did you know," he remarked, "as Companions of the Messenger of Allah ﷺ, whenever we came across a complicated issue, we took it to Aisha because she always had the information that could solve what was puzzling us?"

The congregation marvelled at this, and many students made the effort to visit Aisha in Madinah in order to benefit from her treasure trove of knowledge.

Wealth poured into the Muslim lands during the reign of Umar. The *bayt al-mal*, which was the treasury of the Muslim lands, was overflowing with the finest jewels, money, weaponry, grain and goods. Umar decided to establish a special stipend for the Companions of the Prophet ﷺ who had served the Ummah in its earliest, most difficult times. Umar appointed registrars to account for the zakah and other wealth flowing into Madinah.

"We will establish a system to distribute the wealth to those who worked hardest for the sake of Allah," Umar told his ministers. "I will start with the household of the Messenger of Allah ﷺ. First, the Mothers of the Believers."

And so, Umar sent a regular salary of 10,000 dirhams each to the wives of the Prophet ﷺ. But to Aisha he sent 12,000 dirhams, saying, "She was the beloved of the Messenger of Allah ﷺ."

Once, some gemstones and jewellery arrived in Madinah from Iraq, after one of the Muslim conquests. Umar looked over the jewellery and turned to his companions. "Do you know how much these are worth?" he asked. The Sahaba had never seen such jewels and they shook their heads, uncertain about how to divide the war booty.

"Would you allow me to send it to Aisha?" Umar asked. "For the sake of the Messenger of Allah's ﷺ love for her?" The companions agreed, so he sent the treasure to her.

Aisha shuddered when she saw the cloth bag full of jewels. It was a fortune! Her mind flashed back to her simple life with Rasulullah ﷺ. The little onyx necklace she would borrow and wear was as much jewellery as she had worn for Rasulullah ﷺ. She shook her head.

Why does Umar put me in this position after the death of Rasulullah? Aisha asked herself, worried about the allure of the riches pouring into the Muslim lands.

Then Aisha thought back to the advice she remembered from the Messenger of Allah ﷺ on different occasions:

If you want to be with me in the Hereafter, take only
what a traveller needs from this world.
O Aisha, Do not turn away the needy even if with a piece of date.
O Aisha, Love the needy and be near them.
O Aisha, save yourself from the Hellfire, even if it means
giving just half a date in charity...

"O Allah," Aisha said, her voice trembling. "Please don't let me be left with this gift until tomorrow." Then she instructed her household helpers to give most of the wealth away in charity, saying:

"My Lord, do not give me even one more chance to experience this kind of benevolence. Please take my soul before I see another such gift!"

She didn't want to be dazzled and distracted by worldly temptations and risk losing out on the rewards of the Hereafter.

After some of the conquests, there were many pieces of land to distribute. Umar offered the Mothers of the Believers a choice. They could have a piece of land to have cultivated as a source of income or they could have a monthly allowance. Aisha and Hafsah chose the allowance because it allowed them to give to the poor more easily.

During Umar's rule, people started turning to Aisha for her opinions on different matters, and she began to issue fatwas, which are important rulings in Islam. These fatwas played a big role in shaping the foundations of the Shari'ah, the system of Islamic law.

Senior Companions of the Prophet Muhammad ﷺ often visited Aisha's home to ask her questions, knowing she had a unique understanding of his daily life. Her inquisitive mind had led her to ask many questions during his lifetime, and she had learned much about his Sunnah - his teachings and practices. Her sharp memory and clear, direct way of explaining matters were greatly valued by those who came to seek knowledge.

If she was unsure of the answer, Aisha would direct people to those whom she thought knew better. Once, someone asked about travellers wiping over their socks in *wudu*. "Ask Ali," she replied, "for he was with the Messenger of Allah on most of his journeys."

Umar too, would seek Aisha's help in settling legal matters which were complicated or difficult. He would send his messenger to her home to ask about various practices of the Prophet ﷺ.

Once, Umar's friend gave some rolls of cloth as charity to a group of women who had been involved in immoral activities and were being held outside the city.

"Such charity will surely not be accepted," said Umar, firmly believing he was right. Umar's friend begged to differ, saying that the Prophet ﷺ had said about such outlaws, "The things you give them are considered as charity from you, too."

Umar was angry when he heard this and said this must be a slander against the Prophet ﷺ. They agreed to go to Aisha for a solution. Umar's friend asked Aisha, "O Mother of the Believers, didn't you hear the Messenger of Allah ﷺ saying: 'The things that you give them are considered as charity from you, too'?"

"As Allah is my witness, yes," Aisha replied. "I did indeed hear that." She explained that the Prophet ﷺ had allowed charity to be given to such people since they were poor and it might encourage them to leave their life of crime behind.

This revelation left Umar in shock. "I can't believe how much I missed learning from Allah's Messenger ﷺ," he lamented, "all while I was busy attending to my business!"

One day, Aisha was fasting. Abdullah bin az-Zubayr, her nephew, sent her two sacks full of grain. They were worth a lot of money, so Aisha divided them into bowls and gave them to the poor people of Madinah.

"O *Umm al-Mu'mineen*! Good news!" said Dhakwan, Aisha's servant boy, beaming as he entered the room.

"*Amir al-Mu'mineen* has replied to your message. He has given permission for the wives of Rasulullah ﷺ to go on Hajj this year!"

For years, Umar had not deemed it suitable for the Mothers of the Believers to go on the pilgrimage. They had sent him a request this year, hoping that he would agree.

Aisha wanted to strive to do as many good deeds as she could. Once, she remarked to Rasulullah ﷺ, "O Messenger of Allah, we consider jihad - fighting in the way of Allah - to be the best deed."

"The best jihad for women," the Prophet ﷺ had told her, "is to perform a sinless Hajj." Ever since then, Aisha held his words close to her heart and desired to go for Hajj.

Aisha was beside herself with joy. But now it was sunset and time to break her fast. "Little girl!" she called Umm Dharrah, her servant girl. "Bring me something to break my fast with!"

Umm Dharrah sighed. "O *Umm al-Mu'mineen*, I wish you'd saved some of what was sent to you by your nephew. We could have bought some meat for you to break your fast with."

Aisha rubbed her forehead. "Don't scold me," she replied. "If you had reminded me, I would have done so."

But Aisha was still so full of joy from the news of Hajj that it didn't matter. Hajj season was approaching and there were preparations to be made.

The camels were ready. All eight of them had an identical *hawdaj* constructed on top of them provided by the caliph. Aisha's *hawdaj* today was much stronger and more decorative than the one she had in the days when she travelled with Rasulullah ﷺ. It was like a tall, wooden, pointed tent structure, tightly bound with ropes and covered in decorative fabric curtains. The roof was draped in fabric adorned with tassels. Inside was a special chair with a leather cushion, shaped especially for ladies to sit comfortably atop a camel. It fitted over the top of the camel's hump with bags of luggage secured underneath.

As caliph, Umar was the overall leader of the Hajj. He headed for the caravan departing from Madinah. He appointed Uthman bin Affan to take special care of the Mothers of the Believers during the journey. Uthman's camel guided the contingent of the Mothers of the Believers, who were in their prominent *hawdajs*. As the caravan moved off, those left behind pointed towards the procession, lifting infants onto their shoulders so they could glimpse the grand sight of the Mothers of the Believers riding under their elegant canopies.

"Stay clear, stay clear!" Uthman would call if he saw other travellers getting too close. The great Companion, Abdurrahman bin Awf, volunteered to guard the Mothers of the Believers from the back of their delegation. Aisha was touched by their care for the welfare of the wives of the Prophet ﷺ during the long journey.

On their journey, they camped near Qudayd, not far from where Umm Ma'bad lived. Umm Ma'bad was the lady whose camp the Prophet ﷺ and Abu Bakr had sought refuge in during their Hijrah, years ago. She was known for her generosity towards travellers, and for the vivid, unforgettable description she gave of the Prophet ﷺ: how his face shone with light, how his words flowed like perfectly strung pearls, and how those who sat with him listened with rapt attention, eager to serve him. She watched as Uthman led the camels with their *hawdajs* to a secluded area sheltered by trees, away from the rest of the caravan.

Umm Ma'bad prepared a bowl of meat and a pitcher of milk and headed to the encampment. She asked for permission to enter the tent and, when she had done so, she saw the beautiful faces of the wives of the Prophet ﷺ. The elderly Umm Ma'bad was overcome and began to sob.

"What is making you weep?" they asked her, all at once.

"I remembered the Messenger of Allah," she said between sobs.

The Mothers of the Believers wept. "This was where he took shelter, at my tent..." Umm Ma'bad explained. She handed them food and they accepted graciously.

They all realised who she was and began to embrace and greet her. She had witnessed a miracle with her own eyes - how the Prophet ﷺ had placed his blessed hands upon her frail goat, and by Allah's permission, it had given milk in abundance.

"O Umm Ma'bad," said Aisha, "when we reach our destination, come and visit us, for we each wish to give you a gift when *Amir al-Mu'mineen* gives our stipend to us." Umm Ma'bad nodded her head and smiled at the sentiment.

The Hajj was very special. Aisha circled the Ka'bah, walked between Mount Safa and Marwa, and spent the

days of Mina and Arafah alongside the other Mothers of the Believers. After the rites were completed, and before their return to Madinah, delegations of the Quraysh came to pay their respects to Aisha at the house where she stayed. Her servant, Dhakwan, served as her doorman during her time there and would lead her in prayer.

The news of Zaynab bint Jahsh passing away reached the Mothers of the Believers, filling them with sorrow. It had been nine years since the passing of the Prophet ﷺ. They recounted Zaynab's wonderful qualities and remarked that she was the first of the wives to follow him into the next life.

It all made sense to Aisha now. She recalled a time when they had all asked the Prophet ﷺ who would pass away first, after him. To which he had replied, "The one among you with the longest arm."

The longest arm? The wives had thought. Curious to know who it was, the wives had stretched their arms against the wall to see whose was longest, and it certainly wasn't Zaynab's. But now that she was gone, they realised the Prophet ﷺ meant it in a different way.

Zaynab was skilled at tanning leather and creating beautiful crafts with her hands, which she sold. She always gave her earnings to charity, and everyone knew she was the most giving amongst them - hence she was the one with the longest arm.

"He meant by it: charity!" said Aisha.

Aisha was genuinely happy for Zaynab. The old rivalries and jealousy she once felt had all washed away, replaced by love. Zaynab had stood by her during the darkest moment of her life, when she was slandered, and Aisha knew that her support came from deep *taqwa*, a true consciousness of Allah. Zaynab was undoubtedly a woman of Jannah.

Aisha felt joy in Zaynab's status, knowing she was praised as the most charitable of the wives.

Aisha realised there was no need to compete to be the Prophet's ﷺ favourite, for each wife had her own unique qualities and a special place with Allah and in the heart of His Messenger ﷺ. With that realisation, Aisha's heart was at ease.

CHAPTER 29
'Umar's 'Last Wish

Aisha often reflected on the remarkable changes that took place during the 10 years of Umar bin al-Khattab's caliphate. It was a time when the Muslim Ummah expanded its reach, bringing the light of Islam to new communities and guiding them out of the darkness of worshipping idols and false beliefs. Cities like Jerusalem, Damascus and Baghdad flourished under their nurturing leadership. Those who did not embrace Islam could still remain as citizens under the protection of the Muslims, practising their own religions, having their own courts, and benefiting from the flourishing civilization around them while living in peace and harmony.

During the years of Umar's rule, the message of Islam was spreading far and wide. Time seemed to pass so fast. After Zaynab's death, Mariyah also passed away, and they were both buried in the Baqi cemetery in Madinah. Eight Mothers of the Believers remained: Aisha, Sawdah, Hafsah, Umm Salamah, Juwairiyah, Safiyyah, Umm Habibah and Maymunah.

Umar was more than just a ruler; he was a leader with vision and strength. Aisha noticed how he set up systems of justice and welfare programmes to support those in need, making sure that help reached the hungry and the sick. His government was well-organised, with the caliph at the top, dividing the Muslim lands into provinces overseen by carefully chosen governors called *Walis*. Each province was further split into about 100 districts, managed by junior governors known as *Amirs*. Important roles like the Chief Secretary, Military Secretary, Revenue Collector, Police Chief, Treasury Officer and Chief Judge ensured that everything ran smoothly, creating a strong community where people could live in peace and harmony.

Umar's governor in Shaam was Mu'awiyah, who lived in Damascus - a city the Muslims had conquered from the Byzantines, who were part of the Eastern Roman Empire. As the son of Abu Sufyan, Mu'awiyah was born to lead. His sharp mind, graceful manners and effortless charm won him the deep love and respect of the people of Damascus.

However, as Governor, Mu'awiyah made decisions that were different from the simplicity Umar was known for.

Mu'awiyah built a grand palace in the city's heart, dressed in fine robes, and would hold a procession to announce his presence. This reflected the splendour the people of Damascus were accustomed to under Byzantine rule.

One day, Umar decided to visit Damascus. Mu'awiyah had arranged an impressive procession to welcome him and appeared dressed in fine clothing. When Umar saw the display, he turned to his talented young governor with a firm but curious gaze.

"Are you the one behind this grand display?" Umar asked, his voice calm but laced with concern. "Why do you do this?" he added, objecting to the pomp and ceremony, since the way of the Prophet ﷺ had always been simplicity.

"Yes," replied Mu'awiyah respectfully, and then explained why. "O Commander of the Faithful, the Byzantines ruled the people of Damascus only recently. We are now ruling a land full of enemy spies. To maintain their fear and respect, we must appear strong, wealthy and powerful. But if you forbid me, I will stop."

Umar weighed Mu'awiyah's words carefully. His heart leaned towards simplicity, for that had been the way of the Prophet ﷺ. Yet he saw the sense in Mu'awiyah thinking. Every land had its own culture and a wise ruler knew how to meet the needs of his people. For Mu'awiyah, the display of strength was not for his own pride, but to preserve order and inspire respect among those he governed.

Umar accepted that Mu'awiyah should do whatever he felt was wise and in the best interest of Shaam.

"I neither command you to do it, nor forbid you," Umar said.

When Umar was on his deathbed, he sent the copy of the Quran in his care to the Mother of the Believers, Hafsah. Then he called for his son, Ibn Umar.

"O Abdullah bin Umar!" he said, his voice getting weaker and weaker. "Go to the Mother of the Believers, Aisha, and say, 'Umar bin al-Khattab sends his greetings to you', and request her to allow me to be buried with my two companions in her house."

When Ibn Umar conveyed the message to Aisha, she said, "I wanted my own grave to be here. But today I prefer Umar over myself."

"What news do you have?" Umar asked, when his son returned home.

"O Commander of the Faithful!" Ibn Umar said. "She has given permission."

Umar closed his eyes and exhaled. "Nothing was more important to me than to be buried in that place." But even then, the gallant Umar's brow furrowed. "I fear that she felt pressured to comply because I am *Amir al-Mu'mineen*," he said to Ibn Umar. "So, when I die, carry me to Aisha's house and convey my greetings to her. Then ask her once again with these words: 'Khattab's son, Umar, seeks permission'. Then if she gives permission, bury me there, and if she does not, then take me to the graveyard of the Muslims."

Umar passed away 20 years after the Hijrah following 10 years of rule. When he was buried in her house, Aisha recalled the dream she had mentioned long ago to her father, in which three moons entered her home. With the burial of Umar, she realised the dream had come true and the great Umar was the third moon.

Now that Umar was buried there, Aisha felt shy to take her head coverings off in her house, and so she had a screen fitted in her room that partitioned off the three graves, leaving only a narrow space for her to sleep.

Umar had always been a sincere adviser and well-wisher to the Mothers of the Believers. Even though at times, he was forthright with his advice to them, they all knew he had their best interests at heart.

After Umar's death, his son Ibn Umar moved to Makkah. Whenever he would return to Madinah, he would enter the masjid of the Prophet ﷺ and go towards the special area in the Prophet's ﷺ masjid called the *Rawdah*. Aisha's house, which held the three graves, was right beside it, so Ibn Umar would say, "Peace be upon you, O Messenger of Allah. Peace be upon you, O Abu Bakr. Peace be upon you, O my father." And the Muslims continue to do this today.

CHAPTER 30
Trouble in Madinah

"When Umar passed away and Uthman assumed leadership," Aisha reminisced one day, "Umm Salamah, Maymunah, Umm Habibah and I gathered and sent a message to Uthman, requesting permission to perform Hajj. He responded, 'Umar did as you witnessed.
I will perform Hajj with you, just as Umar used to. Therefore, if any of you wish to perform Hajj, I will accompany her'."

Up until that time, the Quran had mainly been meticulously memorised by the Sahaba and passed down through oral tradition. But as the Muslim community grew and more non-Arabs entered the fold of Islam, Caliph Uthman saw the need for written copies to be distributed throughout the Ummah. He called on Mother of the Believers, Hafsah, for the copy of the Quran that was placed in her safekeeping and had copies made by the experts of Quran among the Sahaba. Each copy was called a *mus-haf* - a written manuscript of the Quran. These *mus-hafs* were sent to the four corners of the Muslim lands to ensure everyone had the same accurate copy to recite, understand and follow.

For several years, Uthman ruled in peace, bringing changes to the Muslim lands that improved people's lives. The message of Islam spread during his reign to North Africa and Central Asia. Many of the newcomers to Islam didn't know the great Sahaba and their role in the life of the Prophet ﷺ, and over time, murmurs of discontent surfaced about the governors who Uthman had appointed.

People began whispering in marketplaces and under shaded trees, claiming these governors were harsh and unjust, asserting they held their positions and wealth only because they were Uthman's relatives.

Rumours, borne on the wind and embellished with each retelling, falsely painted Uthman as favouring his family and relatives. These stories cast shadows on his leadership and false doubts. Murmurs turned into heated discussions in bustling squares, where sceptics openly questioned his leadership. Some critics even believed that Uthman's rule was hurting the unity of the Muslim community, creating an atmosphere filled with suspicion and confusion. Soon, waves of rebels and rabble-rousers began arriving in Madinah.

One day, a messenger arrived at Aisha's home with a question. "O my dear mother," he began respectfully, "some of your children have sent me to you." By 'children', he meant the Muslims, for as a Mother of the Believers, they were all considered her children. "They send their greetings and ask for your opinion on Uthman bin Affan."

The question sent chills down Aisha's spine. Did they not know the status of Uthman in the Prophet's ﷺ eyes? Did they not know his love for Uthman, that the Prophet ﷺ married two of his beloved daughters to him? Or that the Prophet ﷺ had declared that even the angels were in awe of Uthman bin Affan? Did they not understand the sacrifices Uthman and the other Companions had made for the sake of Allah?

"Allah curses anyone who curses Uthman," Aisha said, clearly and unmistakably.

A stormy cloud had cast its shadow over Madinah. The Mothers of the Believers could sense its presence and smell the change in the air. Every day, foreign young men were arriving in droves, and their intentions were unclear.

These men were not like the usual visitors who came to Madinah to pay their respects, offering greetings to the Prophet ﷺ and praying at his masjid. They were coarse, uncultured and vulgar. This rabble roamed the streets like mobsters, shouting and showing disrespect to the remaining Companions. Day after day, they paraded through Madinah, chanting slogans against Uthman. Concerned for his safety, the Companions and their families took action, with Ali, Asma and others sending their sons to take turns guarding Caliph Uthman's house.

Then the day came when the mobsters surrounded Uthman's house and things got more out of hand. There were hundreds of them. They chanted and hurled abuse. Each one of them seemed emboldened by his brother. Before long, Uthman's house was well and truly under siege and riots broke out.

Poor Uthman and his wife were inside the house, with nothing to eat or drink. The Companions could not bear this. The Prophet's ﷺ wife, Umm Habibah, ventured outside to take water to the house of Uthman. Surely the mobsters would not harm her, would they?

But as the crowds grew, with people barging and chanting slogans and no space to move, nobody noticed that Umm Habibah was in their midst carrying a pitcher of water to Uthman's household. Nobody realised that, with emotions running high, the crowd had nearly trampled on the Mother of the Believers, Umm Habibah. Thankfully, she made it home unscathed.

When Aisha heard about the incident, she frowned, shaking her head in dismay at the growing unrest. Yet, there was little time to dwell on it because she would soon begin her pilgrimage to Makkah.

As the caravan set out, the gentle sway of Aisha's *hawdaj*, rocking with the steady pace of the camel beneath her, offered a moment of calm. With the horizon stretching before her, and her co-wives in their *hawdajs* beside her, she extended her hands in prayer, asking Allah for a peaceful and safe return.

Between the Hira and Thabir Mountains on the outskirts of Makkah, Aisha had a house where she would stay during Hajj season. There, delegations would come to meet her and ask her questions. Shaybah bin Uthman was the key bearer of the Ka'bah and his family was responsible for keeping the Ka'bah clean and replacing its *kiswah* cover regularly. When Shaybah heard that the Mother of the Believers was in Makkah, he went to pay his respects.

Shaybah stood near Aisha's dwelling and greeted her. Aisha's servant, Dhakwan, answered the door and one of her nephews was with her. After exchanging some pleasantries, Aisha asked him some questions. "What do you do with the old cloth covering the House of Allah when you replace it with a new one?"

"Well," explained Shaybah, "we bury it in a deep pit so that no one disrespects it or uses it for lowly purposes."

Aisha raised her eyebrows at this. "This is not right," she said. "You are making a mistake. When the cloth is taken off the Ka'bah, it is no longer sacred. It can be used for other things. You should sell the old cloth-covering and spend the money on the poor and needy."

Shaybah leaned forward, nodding humbly and listening through the curtain to *Umm al-Mu'mineen's* correction. When Aisha advised people, they listened because she did so with knowledge and sincerity. From that day to this, they divide and distribute the Ka'bah's cover whenever it is changed.

CHAPTER 31
Assassination

The Hajj season had ended. Aisha sat in her tent on the outskirts of Makkah, her hands raised in *du'a*. Soon, she would return to Madinah with the other Mothers of the Believers, who had also completed their pilgrimage and were now awaiting permission to return home safely.

After Hajj, there were always many pilgrims left behind, their tents still dotted around the pilgrim sites. The distinct camels of the Mothers of the Believers with their *hawdajs*, were the most prominent camels in the caravan. They had been encamped outside Makkah, preparing for the journey home, when suddenly news from Madinah arrived.

A young man lurched into the encampment, his face was sweating and his eyes were red. There appeared to be a kerfuffle amongst the pilgrims and before long, anguished cries of disbelief began rippling through the tent valley.

"What is the news?" people asked one another. "Is Madinah now safe for return?"

Somebody sent a messenger to inform Aisha what had happened.

"*Amir al-Mu'mineen*... they killed him! They killed Uthman!"

When Aisha heard the news, her pulse quickened and she was overcome with disbelief. *How could they?* How had they dared to harm the gentle, noble, forbearing Uthman bin Affan? Did they not realise who he was? He was the son-in-law of the Messenger of Allah ﷺ, one of The 10 Promised Paradise. Did they not know that the Prophet ﷺ had given no less than two of his beloved daughters' hands in marriage to him? Did they know that he had nursed his wife, the Prophet's ﷺ daughter Ruqayyah, in her illness until her passing? *How could they?*

Uthman had been one of the *Sabiqun al-Awwalun* - those who embraced the Prophet's ﷺ message in the early days, decades before these troublemakers were even born! The finest of the sons of Banu Umayyah, how beloved Uthman had been to Rasulullah ﷺ!

He was fasting, they told her; he was reading from his *mus-haf*. The troublemakers besieged Uthman's house and deprived him of water. Then the mob stormed his house and...

Aisha's eyes stung with pain. She asked about Naila, the caliph's wife, but was afraid to hear the answer.

"Naila attempted to save her husband, but in raising her left hand to stop a sword falling on him..."

They all winced.

"She was injured terribly, but she is alive. Uthman was martyred as he read the Quran. He was reading the verse:

'And Allah will be enough for your defence against them;
He is the All-Hearing, the All-Knowing.'"
(Quran, 2:137)

Aisha's heart cried. Had this rabble no fear of Allah that they would attack the likes of Uthman?

"Shame! Shame on them!" people called out.

"Shame on us!" others cried.

"Who were 'they'?"

"Rebels from Egypt and Iraq!" someone else exclaimed.

"They assassinated the caliph!"

More news from Madinah trickled in thick and fast, and people reacted with confused chatter. Aisha closed her eyes in utter disbelief at every new report coming from Madinah. What was wrong with people, that the beloved Companion and son-in-law of the Prophet ﷺ could be treated in this way? The questions continued to mull in Aisha's mind.

The troublemakers who had besieged Uthman's house had entered and killed him. When a messenger came to her tent, she asked him, "What about my brother, Muhammad? Where was he when it happened?" To her relief, she was told that he was not there.

"Your nephew, Abdullah bin az-Zubayr, did his best to defend Uthman by fighting off those who were trying to enter, even with his little brother Urwah looking on, but... there were too many of them."

The people in the caravan gathered outside Aisha's tent, listening for her eloquent insights.

"It was your constant criticism of Uthman that caused this," Aisha said, berating no one in particular. Everyone hung their heads in shame. Every one of them knew that the months of rumour-mongering about Uthman, and unfounded stories of how he was favouring his family members, had caused anger to simmer and discontent to erupt throughout the land.

Suddenly, two horsemen arrived in a thick swirl of dust, with only their eyes visible. One of them tall and dark-skinned, the other with a wheatish complexion. Aisha peered from behind the opening of her tent to see what was happening. She recognised the two men who had arrived with such gusto, since they were none other than her own brothers-in-law, Talha and az-Zubayr.

Talha bin Ubaydillah was the same Companion who had joined Aisha's family on the Hijrah journey all those years ago. Now he was married to Aisha's younger sister, Umm Kulthum. His right arm, however, hung limp and lifeless - a reminder of his bravery at the Battle of Uhud. During the battle, he had protected the Prophet ﷺ with all his strength, but the injuries he suffered left his arm paralysed.

As for az-Zubayr, he was honoured with the title *Hawari* - the disciple of the Prophet ﷺ. He had once been part of Aisha's extended family through his marriage to her sister, Asma, though they had since separated. He remained closely connected to Aisha's family as the father of her beloved nephews, Abdullah and Urwah.

Talha and az-Zubayr greeted the group gathered outside Aisha's tent and joined them.

"What news do you bring?" Aisha called from behind the tent flap.

"O *Umm al-Mu'mineen*, Madinah is in strife," replied az-Zubayr. "The air is poisonous. You cannot possibly return at present."

They had escaped after pledging allegiance to Ali as caliph, leaving Madinah in a sorry state. Believers had turned against one another and the people of Shaam were refusing to pledge allegiance to Ali. Many of them were from the Banu Umayyah clan - Uthman's family - and they were furious. Their kinsman was dead and his killers still at large. Tension hung in the air and something unthinkable loomed on the horizon: Muslims, for the first time in their history, might raise swords against fellow Muslims. The very thought shook the hearts of the Companions.

Aisha sat quietly, searching for the answer. Then she began to recite the verses of the Quran:

> *"And if two groups of Believers fight each other,*
> *then make peace between them. But if one*
> *of them transgresses against the other, then*
> *fight against the transgressing group until*
> *they submit to the rule of Allah. If they do so, then*
> *make peace between both groups in all fairness and*
> *act justly. Surely Allah loves those who uphold justice.*
> *The Believers are but onc brotherhood, so make*
> *peace between your brothers. And be mindful*
> *of Allah so you may be shown mercy."*
> (Quran, 49:9-10)

"How firmly people need to hold on to these verses now!" Aisha proclaimed. The crowd listened to the wise words of the Mother of the Believers.

Due to the unrest in Madinah, Aisha's caravan packed their belongings, and many turned back and stayed in Makkah. As they entered the valley of Makkah and made their way into the city, Aisha knew exactly where she wanted to go. Her camel was lowered and she stepped out of her *hawdaj* as people looked on. She walked over to the Ka'bah, to the

Hijr Ismail, the wall of stone erected to mark the place where the original Ka'bah wall had been. There, Aisha fell down in prostration, weeping for the Ummah. People gathered sombrely, their faces gloomy and shoulders hunched, waiting for her to speak.

"O people," said Aisha. "Uthman, the Commander of the Faithful, has been killed. They spread such lies about him, when in fact he was as pure as gold, as clean as clothes washed in spring water, and he was a man who would stand in prayer with dignity and purity. How is it possible for us to allow the bloodshed of our leader? However many they are in number, these rebels are not equal to even one finger of Uthman."

Her words affected the people, each face deep in thought.

"How could Uthman have been killed so brutally and so easily?" one man asked.

"We shall not leave Makkah, nor shall we return home, until the murderers of Uthman are found and brought to justice!" another proclaimed. The crowd roared with approval.

As Aisha returned to her tent, the air was thick with uncertainty. The wound left by Uthman's killing ran deep, and no one could say if the Ummah would ever heal from the loss of Uthman.

CHAPTER 32
Justice for Uthman

Far away in Damascus, the richly dressed Governor Mu'awiyah, haunted by the killing of his cousin, Uthman, rose from his seat. His face was etched with the turmoil of grief mixed with a simmering anger as he paced restlessly around his *majlis*. Mu'awiyah's *majlis* was a grand room in his Damascene palace, usually reserved for meetings with messengers and dignitaries. Occasionally, he paused, his eyes fixing on the intricate patterns on the walls as if they might hold answers.

"Couldn't you have done anything to help him? Not a thing?" Mu'awiyah pressed, his voice heavy with distress.

The military officer standing before him remained silent, his eyes fixed on the wall beyond his commander, his face motionless and defeated.

Mu'awiyah thought he'd acted swiftly when trouble erupted in Madinah, sending a small army to guard his cousin Uthman's house. However, the effort turned out to be futile; Uthman had been martyred before help could arrive.

"Sire," the officer replied in a sombre tone, "we had only reached halfway when news of his martyrdom reached us. He met his fate while we were en route."

Stepping outside onto his balcony, Mu'awiyah stared blankly past the lively scene below. Amidst the vibrant tapestry of the old city, Roman architectural remnants, including grand columns and archways, blended seamlessly with Islamic artistry. Simple masjids, with their functional designs and open courtyards, rose among the ancient Roman structures, while minarets emerged, announcing the call to prayer. Alongside these buildings stood venerable old churches and monasteries, silent narrators of the city's Byzantine past. But today, everything he looked upon had lost its lustre.

Mu'awiyah's city was a mosaic of cultures living harmoniously together. Jews, Christians and Muslims coexisted peacefully as citizens within their vibrant and distinct quarters. Their shaven beards and short hair easily distinguished Christian men. Christian women wore long robes and covered their heads like the Muslim women, but left their necks and earrings visible.

Muslim men were characterised by their glistening long beards and smart tunics with embroidered *bisht* cloaks. They sported caps or turbans as headwear. Muslim women veiled themselves, concealing both their bodies and adornments with elegant outer garments when outside. Jewish people could be distinguished by their head coverings and stripy tallit shawls.

Mu'awiyah blinked back a tear and shook his head, his heart heavy with grief and guilt. *I failed him! My dear cousin Uthman... was your blood so cheap?* Mu'awiyah's heart lamented as he buried his head in his hands. *I shall not fail you again.*

It pained Mu'awiyah deeply to hear what had been done to Uthman. *Had they really surrounded his home, denying him food and water?* Mu'awiyah's heart cried as he pictured his cousin sitting quietly, reciting the Quran, when the attackers stormed in - his blood spilling on the very pages he loved. And his wife, injured while trying to shield him... how could it have come to this?

Mu'awiyah clenched his fists. His heart was heavy, but his mind was clear. Justice would have to be served.

Justice, however, would not come easily. With the people of Arabia in disarray and Madinah still reeling from the chaos, the murderers of Uthman, and the few thousand who had backed them, slipped into the shadows. Some fled north to the city of Basra in Iraq; others crept into Ali's army, disguising themselves as loyal soldiers.

People flocked to pledge allegiance to Ali as the new caliph, placing their faith in his ability to bring law and order to the Ummah. His cousin, az-Zubayr, had pledged allegiance, as had Talha, before leaving Madinah. Aisha's younger brother, Muhammad, became Ali's loyal lieutenant, playing a pivotal role in maintaining the army's organisation. People looked to these warriors and seasoned leaders as pillars of strength and stability during a tumultuous time.

Ali feared that the Ummah would be disunited. He felt he needed more time to bring factions together and begin establishing his authority as caliph over the turbulent Muslim lands. His resolve to bring Uthman's killers to justice was unwavering, but he also had to address the many who had voiced their grievances against Uthman, and in certain instances, aligned with his murderers.

While Ali was determined to bring Uthman's killers to justice, he faced a tough choice regarding the many who had protested against Uthman, and those who even supported his killers. Taking a heavy-handed approach could cause civil war to erupt at any moment, reignite unrest, and exacerbate the situation. On top of that, the Roman Empire, ever watchful for opportunities, could exploit any perceived weakness among the Muslims. Ali knew he had to tread carefully.

The Arabian Peninsula and its surrounding areas were in turmoil. Some of the Banu Umayyah, and chief amongst them,

Mu'awiyah, were still refusing to pledge allegiance to Ali until they saw action. They wanted swift justice and reassurances from Ali that the killers were in his sights.

The murderers of Uthman - along with the mobs that had supported them - had escaped justice. And worse still, it was unfolding right before their eyes. *How could they allow such an outrage?* the Banu Umayyah wondered. Something had to be done.

Back in Makkah, Aisha was confined to the encampment of the Mothers of the Believers. They couldn't return to Madinah until calm had been restored. Before long, an increasing number of discontented individuals from across the Arabian Peninsula began arriving in Makkah. Four months had gone by since Uthman had been killed. Daily, disgruntled delegations from every region visited Aisha, and former Banu Umayyah governors, whom Ali had removed, also came to see her.

Talha felt weighed down by guilt. He had come to Makkah, away from the troublemakers who had overrun Madinah, to formulate a plan of action. "I fell short with regards to Uthman," he confessed to Aisha. "How can I be forgiven except by striving to avenge his blood?"

"We must raise an army and restore order and authority in the land," Talha proposed.

Az-Zubayr nodded in agreement, expressing concern that chaos would prevail if Uthman's killers were left unpunished and that there would be no deterrent against such wrongdoing in the future.

"Let's march to Madinah and protest against the injustice to regain authority," someone suggested.

"No, no! We must march upon Basra, where the rebels came from. They are sure to be hiding there. We must go there and demand from the governor that they be handed over for trial."

"Once justice is done, peace and order will follow."

"Careful!" Aisha interjected. "You must be like the better of the two sons of Adam and not draw your swords. You must go with the intention to enjoin the good and forbid the evil."

"O Mother Aisha," said one man, "will you not join us on the journey? Your presence would strengthen our cause and would help maintain peace. Since you are the wife of the Messenger of Allah ﷺ, when people see your *hawdaj*, they will know that we have only peaceful intentions and will desist from any talk of fighting."

"Yes indeed! You will be a unifying force for the Believers, O Mother of the Believers," other voices chimed in. "No one will dare draw a sword when you are among us."

Messengers conveyed similar requests to Hafsah and the other wives of the Prophet ﷺ, encouraging them to join the march to Basra. However, Hafsah's brother, Ibn Umar, now a wise scholar, firmly intervened, forbidding Hafsah from embarking on any such journey.

"You are not to accompany them," he insisted. "As your brother, I will prevent you from going for your own safety." Hafsah heeded her brother's advice and opted to stay in Makkah until the trouble in Madinah had eased. This could take quite a few months.

With no sign of return to Madinah, and the Muslim community teetering on the brink of civil war, Aisha thought long and hard. The question that came to her when her father had passed away came to her again: *What is Allah asking of me now?*

One day, while Talha and az-Zubayr were loading their camels and a group of 600 assembled to prepare for their march, a messenger appeared.

"*Umm al-Mu'mineen* has sent word that she will join you on this journey. Perhaps Allah will bring about reconciliation among the Believers through her presence. Uthman was slain wrongfully and by Allah, I shall certainly seek justice for his blood!"

"*Allahu Akbar*!" erupted the cheers of approval. "We let him down in life! By Allah, we will not let him down in death!"

Talha shared a look of quiet satisfaction with az-Zubayr. Both were aware that Aisha's presence would be symbolic and greatly enhance their mission.

"To Basra!" Talha declared, with renewed resolve.

CHAPTER 33
The Dogs of Haw'ab

News travelled fast that the Messenger of Allah's ﷺ wife was marching with an army towards Basra. Speculation was rife that the assassins had hidden there. Men from far and wide, fueled by indignation and a thirst for justice for Uthman, flocked to join the campaign.

Talha and az-Zubayr were at the forefront of the procession. Their every stride was full of determination, their hearts raw in their desire to ensure that the killing of Uthman would not go unavenged. Aisha's camel strode boldly amidst the steady cadence of camels and horses. Her *hawdaj*, draped in its rich, colourful fabrics, was like a lighthouse, guiding the way through a sea of desert beasts.

CHAPTER 33

The trek across the desert was exhausting for the protesters, but they edged closer and closer by the day. When they reached the three-quarter mark of their journey, they stopped for a much-needed rest at an oasis located southwest of Basra.

Someone instructed Aisha's camel to kneel; four young men lifted and carried down her *hawdaj*, allowing her finally to step out, retreat into a tent and stretch her legs.

Aisha could smell the smoky campfires and see their flames dancing in the dark. A light, refreshing breeze made her veil flutter, revealing a desert bathed in moonlight beneath a star-strewn sky. She stood in the desolate darkness, lost in reverie, when she heard a strange sound.

As the breeze continued to play with her veil, Aisha's ears tuned into a distant but rising howl. "What is that?" she whispered to herself, a quiver in her voice as the peculiar sounds intensified.

The air carried an untamed chorus of canine cries, a mixture of sharp barks and stretched howls that filled the night with their wild symphony.

Hooooowwwwl, ruff, ruff, growwwwwll, the sounds echoed.

Aisha looked around frantically, raising the alarm. Az-Zubayr and his companions hastened towards her tent, wondering what the commotion was about.

THE DOGS OF HAW'AB

"Where have we reached?" Aisha called out through the canvas of her tent.

"We are near the pond of Haw'ab," one of the men replied, leaning closer to the tent's entrance.

"Haw'ab, you say?" Aisha's heart raced, goosebumps prickling her skin. She was short of breath. "Oh no!" she cried, "I implore you; we must return at once!"

The men stood next to her tent, looking at each other, perplexed. "But why, O Mother of the Believers?" one of them inquired. "What agitates you so? It is just the sound of dogs barking at their own shadows. We are nearing the end of our journey."

"Yes, you must continue with us," agreed Talha, "for when the Muslims see you, Allah will bring peace between them through you."

The stars above appeared to dim and Aisha closed her eyes, overwhelmed by a sense of impending doom as the dreadful barking echoed in her ears. Then she explained her agitation.

"Allah's Messenger ﷺ once said to us - his wives - 'One of you will come to her senses when she hears the dogs of Haw'ab barking'." Aisha explained, with worried urgency in her voice. "It appears he meant me!"

Talha and az-Zubayr pleaded with Aisha to continue the journey. When no one was around, Aisha scrambled out of her tent and stood alone with only the black tent of night surrounding her. In the pitch-black darkness, her *jilbab* billowed out behind her in the desert wind.

Nobody saw the desperate, solitary figure with tears streaming down her face, engulfed in isolation. Nobody could perceive the sharp pain of uncertainty gnawing at the pit of her stomach. Aisha stared into the bleak, harsh terrain of the desert stretching before her. It was an endless abyss, leading to nowhere.

How she longed for the Prophet's ﷺ counsel, for his voice to steady her trembling heart. How she yearned to run to her father, to cling to his certainty and feel his guiding hand once more.

They would know.

They would care.

They always had.

She must cling to the strongest handhold - the one she had always had: her trust in Allah. Aisha prayed for guidance. As dawn beckoned, her tears dried up and the ghastly barking of the dogs of Haw'ab waned until it finally ceased.

There was no turning back now.

CHAPTER 34
Ali Takes a Stand

By the time the protesters reached the city's boundaries, their numbers had swelled from 600 to a staggering 30,000.

Ali, the new caliph, was at his headquarters in Madinah when he received word of their march. The mobsters' revolts against Uthman had already plunged Muslim lands into chaos. And now this? Ali shook his head in disbelief. This was the last thing he needed.

In the province of Shaam, Mu'awiyah and the Banu Umayyah clan had already refused to pledge allegiance to Ali until the killers of Uthman had been brought to justice. Ali feared that the Ummah was divided. The burden of upholding order and keeping the Ummah united rested heavily on his shoulders. It was crucial for Ali to regain control now.

Basra stood as Ali's stronghold in Iraq, firmly under his authority. However, the tens of thousands of marchers, led by Talha and az-Zubayr and accompanied by Aisha, were now gathering at the city's gates. He feared their presence might undermine his leadership and he knew he couldn't allow them to enter Basra unchallenged.

"Tell the Governor to prevent them from entering the city," Ali instructed his messenger. "I am not certain what Talha, az-Zubayr and Mother of the Believers, Aisha, are intending." And with that, the messenger jumped onto a horse and sped towards Iraq.

Upon receiving Ali's message, the Governor of Basra dispatched his soldiers to defend the city. However, many of his soldiers abandoned their posts and joined the marchers accompanying Aisha. Ka'b, the Judge of Basra, equally outraged by Uthman's assassination, left the city to join Aisha's group.

The Governor of Basra was furious but couldn't stop them, and so the marchers entered the city with little resistance. In a panic, the Governor sent a messenger to Ali. "30,000 have entered the city with Aisha in their ranks. I cannot resist their entry! You must come to Basra at once!"

Aisha's camel entered Basra, surrounded by the mass of protesters, who began setting up camp. The caravan ceased to be a caravan and became a disorderly tangle of tents, men, camels, horses, baggage and noise.

Back in Madinah, Ali was anxious and had called a meeting of his viziers. "We need someone who has experience in both war and diplomacy," one of them said.

"Bring me Qa'qa!" Ali demanded suddenly, summoning the trusty general to his chamber. Qa'qa bin Amr was a formidable warrior who'd participated in many battles under the caliphs.

"Yes, O Commander of the Faithful!" replied Qa'qa when he arrived, standing tall and alert. His broad shoulders were clad in armour, his sturdy body covered in chain-mail. Qa'qa held his polished silver helmet in his arm so that for once the wavy black hair framing his face was visible.

"You must go ahead of me and negotiate with the marchers encircling Basra. Speak to Talha, az-Zubayr and Aisha and find a peaceful resolution."

Qa'qa nodded in obedience.

"And do ask Talha," Ali continued, "how does it please him that his wife is at home, safe and sound, while the Mother of the Believers - the wife of Rasulullah ﷺ - has embarked on this dangerous journey?"

Ali sighed. "I will be hot on your heels with my men following close behind you."

CHAPTER 35
The Catastrophic Incident of the Camel

When Qa'qa arrived in Basra, he found a large encampment insidc the gates of the city. The air was thick with tension as armoured men moved through the camp, bracing for whatever might come next. Qa'qa walked steadily among the crowded rows of tents, their poles hastily driven into the ground, their canvases flapping restlessly in the wind.

He requested an audience with Aisha, who had settled in a large tent in the middle of the encampment. Her voice was strong and confident when she spoke to male delegates, even though they couldn't see her. The tent was simple but nice, with woven mats on the ground and lanterns giving off a warm, glowing light.

"My mother, what is the matter? Why have you come here?" Qa'qa asked, his tone respectful yet urgent.

"We have come to avenge the death of Uthman," Aisha replied firmly. "We wish to punish the culprits and reconcile the Ummah. That is all."

"And how will you achieve that reconciliation and peace?" Qa'qa inquired, trying to understand the depth of their intentions.

"By avenging Uthman's murder and punishing his murderers and their supporters," she explained. "This is to establish justice, as the Quran commands us."

"The culprits are hiding in homes all over Basra and some of them have joined Ali's army!" someone interjected, their voice tense with anger.

"That is not confirmed," Qa'qa responded. "By punishing 600, you will unleash 6,000 people wanting revenge. This will not lead to peace."

Qa'qa looked into the faces of the men gathered around Aisha's tent. "Isn't it better to wait for the turmoil to calm," he reasoned, "as the Caliph Ali has commanded, so that people may be brought to justice in an orderly fashion?"

Then Qa'qa turned to Talha and az-Zubayr, who stood nearby, their faces tense. "Talha, az-Zubayr, you have already pledged allegiance to Ali, so what brings you here against his wishes?"

"Our sole objective is to punish Uthman's murderers and set matters right," Talha explained, his voice steady.

"To bring about reconciliation," az-Zubayr added, nodding in agreement.

Qa'qa looked at them sympathetically. *"Amir al-Mu'mineen* Ali is committed to finding the culprits, but he is waiting for the right moment to avoid unnecessary bloodshed."

Aisha considered Qa'qa's words, the silence in the tent heavy with contemplation.

"You're right," she said eventually, her voice softer but resolute. "You have spoken the truth. Go and tell Ali that if he shares this opinion then the matter is settled because peace is of utmost importance."

By the time Ali arrived in Basra, 20,000 men had joined his army. They camped outside the city, their tents stretching across the horizon, mirroring the rival encampment.

The night was alive with the noise of men preparing for potential confrontation, the soft glow of campfires revealing faces that were both worn and resolute.

Ali observed Qa'qa arriving at his camp after three days of negotiations. Curious about the outcome, he awaited Qa'qa's report. When Ali heard the requests of the marchers, he was happy to agree to the terms. Among the commitments made were:

1. That the caliph must remove the troublemakers from around Madinah.
2. That he must expel from his own camp anyone who had shown sympathy or support for the assassination of Uthman.
3. That the caliph must find and punish those individuals who were directly involved in Uthman's assassination.

As night fell, both camps went to sleep, satisfied an agreement had been reached, and that they would soon be heading home.

Nobody noticed the skulking figures in the dead of night who had been hiding within their ranks all this time. Nobody heard their breathless whispers and muffled tread.

Swish, swish! Tens of daggers worked diligently in the night. *Swish, slashhh!*

The troublemakers had infiltrated both camps, moving with deadly precision. In the chilling quiet of dawn, the grisly truth was unveiled - people woke up to find their brothers dead in both camps, victims of a ruthless slaughter under the cover of darkness. Panic erupted as each side confronted the grim reality of betrayal.

Aisha's camp awoke to the horrifying sight of their fallen comrades, their lifeless bodies testifying to the treachery that had unfolded in the night. Meanwhile, Ali's camp was in utter disbelief at the loss of men killed in their sleep. Anger and suspicion spread like wildfire, fanned by fear and confusion.

"Betrayal! Betrayal!" the cries rang out from both sides, accusations mingling with cries of mourning. Suddenly, fighting erupted, transforming the once tranquil camps into a battlefield of chaos and despair.

For the first time, Muslims drew swords against fellow Muslims. Ali, desperate to stop the bloodshed, moved through the fray, calling for peace. Aisha stood nearby, her pulse racing, her heart heavy with sorrow and helplessness as she witnessed the carnage unfolding before her eyes.

Blades whistled through the air, striking each other with sharp clangs. Shouts of men soared up to the sky, mingling with cries of anguish, the thunder of hooves and the whinnying of stallions. The fighting continued relentlessly, killing thousands in the chaos.

Talha, astride his horse, galloped frantically across the battlefield, his voice straining to rise above the clash of arms. "Sheathe your swords!" he cried, the words torn from him in desperation.

An arrow whistled through the air, finding its mark with a sickening thud. Talha's face contorted in agony as the

arrow struck his thigh. Blood flowed freely from the wound, staining the ground a dark red. The bleeding wouldn't stop and Talha collapsed.

Ali confronted az-Zubayr, pulling his cousin's face so close that he could see the whites of his eyes. "Do you remember, O Cousin," Ali exclaimed, "when the Prophet ﷺ told you that one day there would be a dispute between us and that you would be in the wrong?"

Az-Zubayr's eyes widened in recognition and waves of remorse crashed over him. He withdrew from the

battlefield, his heart heavy with regret. Unbeknownst to him, a shadow slipped from the edge of the battlefield, silently trailing his steps.

Across the battlefield, Ka'b, the Judge of Basra, approached Aisha with a daring suggestion to end the chaos. "Mother of the Believers," he implored, "if you ride forth with your *hawdaj,* perhaps the sight of your presence will move them to lay down their arms and seek peace!"

Aisha did not know what to do. She led her camel into the middle of the battlefield where everyone could see her *hawdaj.*

Soldiers encircled her like a ring of iron, rushing to protect the Prophet's ﷺ wife. But alas, the fighting continued.

Without warning, something sharp pierced her *hawdaj*.

Thunk!

An arrow had struck - then another, and another.

Thunk, thunk, thunk! They tore into the protective canvas one after another. Inside, Aisha froze, shrinking from the menacing arrowheads that were poking through. It was a sorrowful sight - her *hawdaj*, once a symbol of honour and dignity, was now bristling with arrows like the spines of a wounded hedgehog.

Seated on his horse, Ali watched from afar, his heart sinking as the scene unfolded. Fear gnawed at him, knowing Aisha was in grave danger amidst the tumultuous battlefield. Beside him, on horseback, Muhammad bin Abi Bakr, Aisha's brother, sat in solemn silence, his eyes fixed on his sister's camel.

"We must bring down her camel to end this," Ali declared, his brow glistening with sweat, his voice firm, the blazing Mesopotamian sky burning in his eyes.

The men hesitated for a moment at the audacious plan. Bringing down the Mother of the Believers' revered camel seemed unthinkable. But they had no choice.

Charging in from behind, they struck at the camel's hind legs. Aisha felt the sudden impact from inside the *hawdaj*, but her senses were overwhelmed, confusing her about what was happening. Within moments, the camel stumbled and collapsed forward, the *hawdaj* plummeting to the ground with a resounding crash of dust and sand. The cacophony of clashing weapons came to an abrupt end and an eerie silence cloaked the battlefield.

Muhammad bin Abi Bakr charged towards the *hawdaj* and thrust his arm inside the opening of the little tent, startling Aisha.

"Whose insolent hand is this?" she demanded, alarmed at the armoured limb, its hand covered in fine dark hair, that had invaded her *hawdaj*.

"I am your brother, Muhammad," came the response. "Sister, are you uninjured?" Words failed Aisha as she took her brother's hand. He lifted her out of the *hawdaj* and carried her to safety.

When the dust had settled, Ali paced around the battlefield in distress. "Your cousin az-Zubayr is dead," one of Ali's men informed him. "He was leaving the battlefield, not wanting to fight, and then they followed and struck him down." Ali closed his eyes and shook his head. When he opened his eyes again, they were angry.

"Give tidings of Hellfire to the killers of Ibn Safiyyah! My dear cousin! My dear brother...!"

As he paced around inspecting the carnage, he saw Talha, his unarmoured body lying lifeless, and let out a cry. Kneeling down, Ali lifted his beloved brother in faith tenderly in his arms and wiped the dust from his face with his own falling tears. "O Talha!" Ali cried. "How I wish I had died before this day!"

Ali came closer to the tent they had erected for Aisha and saw Muhammad bin Abi Bakr leaving. Standing outside her tent, Ali was speechless for a moment.

"*Assalamu alaykum*, Mother of the Believers," Ali said. "It didn't need to come to this." His voice was heavy with regret. The deaths of Talha and az-Zubayr weighed upon his heart.

Inside the tent, Aisha wept salt tears. She never meant for this chaos and bloodshed. Regret gnawed at her for leaving the safety of the four corners of her home in Madinah. She recognised Ali's voice well and crept closer to the entrance flap.

For decades, he'd been her neighbour; he was family. If only they were meeting in different circumstances. "*Wa alaykumussalam wa rahmatullahi wa barakatuhu*, O Commander of the Faithful," Aisha replied meekly.

Ali and Aisha stood in silence, their hearts yearning for the Prophet's ﷺ wise counsel. But the grim reality in front of them was more like a chilling nightmare and the weight of the whole Muslim Ummah was on their shoulders.

The 'Incident of the Camel', as it became known, was an utter catastrophe. But there was no use in mourning it now.

Ali's mind returned to a moment, many moons ago, when the Messenger of Allah ﷺ had fixed his gaze on him and spoken words he could never forget:

"Someday a matter will arise between you and Aisha..." the Prophet ﷺ had said to Ali, "...when that happens, return her to her place of safety."

Today, Ali would honour the Prophet's ﷺ command and ensure Aisha's safe return home.

"May Allah forgive you," said Ali, all other words failing him. Aisha choked up, unable to find the words to express the anguish in her soul.

"May Allah forgive you too," she said, her voice a hoarse whisper. "I... I only intended reconciliation."

Ali nodded, because he knew.

CHAPTER 36
The Long Road Back

Aisha found it impossible to sleep that night, wondering what she was supposed to do. Her scarf was soaked with tears. Talha was dead! With what face would she greet her poor widowed sister, Umm Kulthum? Az-Zubayr was dead! Even when Aisha tried to rest her eyes, the faces of her orphaned nephews and nieces haunted her.

Ali vacated the largest house in Basra for Aisha and her entourage. It was a magnificent building belonging to a wealthy man in the city, adorned with intricate carvings on the walls, plush cushioned couches and exquisitely crafted wooden furniture. They provided Aisha with everything she needed. Yet, Aisha barely noticed the surrounding opulence, as her world felt treacherously colourless. Her weathered face appeared distant and troubled to those around her.

"How I wish I had been a tree," Aisha sobbed in the privacy of her chamber, thinking about how her call to Basra had led to this: Muslims fighting fellow Muslims for the first time. How upset the Prophet ﷺ would have been to see such a thing. All the water of the Euphrates River couldn't wash away the blessed spilt blood of Believers. "How I wish I was a rock or a pebble... gone and forgotten!"

Rumours began to spread about tensions between Ali and Aisha. Some people were blaming Aisha for the Incident of the Camel. Ali was stern in his response. "A hundred lashes," Ali declared, "for anyone who speaks ill of the Mother of the Believers!"

"Ali is the most auspicious of men," Aisha said to all those around her. "And I only wish goodness and well-being for him," Aisha said, addressing the rumours. "Surely there is no problem between me and Ali any more than the normal little things that exist between a woman and her in-laws."

When Ali heard about Aisha's words, he agreed. "She speaks the truth and by Allah, how beautifully she expresses it!" he said. "She is indeed the wife of your Prophet ﷺ in this world and in the Hereafter."

"O my children!" Aisha cried, addressing anyone who would listen. "Sadly, we hurt one another and endured painful experiences, leaving us all exhausted. Let us draw a line under this today. Let no one look at another with hatred or argue over past actions and harsh words."

The procession proceeded from Basra with all the sombreness of a royal funeral. 40 noble ladies of Basra flanked Aisha's *hawdaj*, like a cortège, as it made its way back to Hijaz, the region where the holy cities were, ready for pilgrimage season once again. Surrounding them were the finest men of Ali's army, and at the forefront, Aisha's brother, Muhammad, led the caravan like a chief pallbearer guiding the way. Inside the *hawdaj*, the shrouded figure of Aisha braced herself for the long journey to Makkah. She would perform Hajj before her return to the city of her beloved Madinah.

During Hajj season, Aisha said to her attendants, "When Ibn Umar passes by, let me know."

Before long, he came to meet her in her Makkah home.

She was still heavy with grief after the incidents in Basra. How fortunate Hafsa had been that her brother Ibn Umar had stopped her from making that wretched journey, as Allah had entrusted the Muslim men with responsibility over the women of their families: to guide them, advise them, and guard them from harm.

"O Abu Abd al-Rahman," she said, using his *kunya*, "why did you not stop me from that march, as you stopped your sister?"

Ibn Umar could only sigh. "Because I saw that another man had already convinced you," he replied with sadness, as he thought of az-Zubayr.

It had been two long years since Aisha had seen her old home and she dreaded the thought of being in the presence of the Prophet's ﷺ grave again, after everything that had just happened. The words of Allah seemed crystal clear now. Allah had instructed the wives of the Prophet ﷺ in the Quran, thus:

O Wives of the Prophet...
Abide in your houses, and make not a dazzling display,
like that of the former Times of Ignorance;
and establish regular Prayer, and give
regular Charity; and obey Allah and His Messenger.

And Allah only wishes to remove all
abomination from you, O members of the Family,
and to make you pure and spotless.
And remember what is recited in your houses
of the verses of Allah and wisdom.
Indeed, Allah is ever Subtle and Aware.
(Quran, 33:32 & 33:34)

It was crystal clear to Aisha that Allah had not made her the youngest wife of the Prophet ﷺ without reason. She had not spent those years with the Prophet ﷺ, asking him questions and learning so much from him, without cause. She knew things about the Messenger of Allah ﷺ that only a wife could know. Indeed, she was one of the only wives of the Prophet ﷺ in whose home verses of the Quran were revealed. Muslims of future generations would need that knowledge to follow in the Prophet's ﷺ footsteps and fulfil the commands of Allah.

She pondered Allah's words and the instructions He had given to the wives of the Prophet ﷺ, searching her soul for answers. And at last, it was clear to her what path would be most pleasing to Allah. She knew what He was asking of her.

Urwah bin az-Zubayr was the teenage son of Asma and much younger than his elder brother, Abdullah, who'd accompanied their father to Basra. He was a bright, curious boy, who usually had a cheery countenance. A studious young man, he sought out the Companions of the Prophet ﷺ and hung on their every word. He would learn from his own mother and often attended the gatherings of the great scribe, Zayd bin Thabit, as well as the Companion, Abu Hurayrah.

"Come, O Urwah," his friends would say. "Come, let us play and make merry!" To which he would shake his head.

"Why don't you seek knowledge too, my friends?" Urwah would respond. "Look at the Sahaba. They are the elders now, but soon they will pass and then we will be the elders. It will be our duty to teach this knowledge!"

Today, Urwah was speeding home through the alleyways of Madinah to his mother. His smile absent and with eyes downcast, he buried his tears in his mother's arms. News of his father az-Zubayr's death had spread throughout the Peninsula and finally reached him. Urwah's mother, Asma, consoled him, reminiscing in hushed tones about the great az-Zubayr and the years they had shared. He had stood by the Prophet ﷺ from the very beginning - brave, loyal and beloved.

By now, Urwah had heard that his aunt, Aisha, was heading back to Madinah. He had not seen her for years and had almost forgotten her face. He looked forward to her return.

CHAPTER 37
Newfound Purpose

Hajj season was over and Muhammad bin Abi Bakr delivered his sister safely home. When Aisha entered Madinah, her camel weaved through its narrow alleyways to her old home. Her brother, Muhammad, jumped back onto his horse and prepared to leave.

"Where to, my brother?" Aisha asked. "Won't you stay a while?"

"I'm off to the land of the Nile," said Muhammad excitedly. "Ali has made me Governor of Egypt, and my men await my arrival." Aisha nodded with understanding, though her heart felt uneasy.

With a lump in her throat, she alighted and walked slowly across the familiar courtyard. She swallowed hard and gently pushed open the door to her house. It felt like a lifetime since she had been within these four walls. Gazing downward, Aisha stood before the screen that separated her from the graves of her husband, her father and the great Umar.

When they were alive, the Prophet's ﷺ wisdom, Abu Bakr's leadership and Umar's firm grip had kept the Ummah from internal strife. She wished she could tell them what had become of the Ummah since their passing.

They were also no longer here *for her*. Aisha's lips trembled as she fought to keep her composure, the sadness etched deeply into her features. She could no longer pester the Prophet Muhammad ﷺ to satisfy her curiosity, nor seek her father's guidance, nor consult Umar. But that was the nature of the world Allah had created.

The passage of time paused for no one. Each generation rose to its peak and departed this earthly realm, making room for the next. There was no turning back, not for the first man, Adam, nor for the final Prophet Muhammad ﷺ, nor for anyone else. Time waited for no one.

Like a relay race, each generation had to take their turn, passing the baton to the next who would carry it forward. The race would continue until the Day of Judgment. What mattered most was running your lap well.

Aisha said a silent prayer. Her longing turned to gratitude as she reflected upon the many years she was devoted to the Prophet ﷺ and how much she had learned from being in his company. Few had spent as much time with him, and even fewer had witnessed his way of life as she had. The words of the Quran revealed for the Mothers of the Believers came back to her again and again:

And recite what is rehearsed in your houses
of the verses of Allah and Wisdom. Indeed,
Allah is ever Subtle and Aware.
(Quran, 33:34)

The answer had been in front of her all along! The Quran and Sunnah - the two guiding lights the Prophet ﷺ had entrusted to them. It was undoubtedly her duty to pass on all she had learned from the verses of Allah - the Quran - and the Wisdom - the Sunnah - which included the sayings, actions, and example of the Prophet ﷺ, to the Believers and preserve it for future generations. The unstoppable passage of time required it. From now on, that would be her purpose.

I swear as long as there is breath in me,
In your footsteps will I traverse patiently,
Defend your name and fulfil your every plea,
Spread your call to all of humanity,
Striving, longing for the day I may be,
United in your blessed company.

"May Allah have mercy upon the women of the Ansar!" Aisha remarked, her soft cheery eyes looking intently at each of the bright, promising young faces in front of her. "For their shyness never prevented them from seeking knowledge."

A crowd of children sat in rows, some orphans, other children of the Companions. Among them were Aisha's own nephews and nieces, Urwah in the front row, Aisha bint Talha by her aunt's elbow, ready to assist her in any way she could. Amrah, a particularly bright student, sat in the line of children too, eager to absorb the teachings of the esteemed Mother of the Believers.

Behind the rows of children sat the ladies. Then there was a curtain, beyond which sat any men who were attending. Each of them was eager to learn from the eloquent Mother of the Believers. Their rows spilled out into the *hujrah*.

"You can ask me anything you like, my dear children," Aisha would say to children and adults alike. "Ask just as you would ask your mother."

"O *Umm al-Mu'mineen*, what did the Messenger of Allah ﷺ sleep upon?"

"The mattress of the Messenger of Allah ﷺ was a tanned skin stuffed with palm fibres," Aisha explained.

"O *Umm al-Mu'mineen*, what did the Messenger of Allah ﷺ eat?"

"The family of Muhammad ﷺ never ate their fill of wheat bread for three consecutive nights, ever since they had come to Madinah, until he passed away."

One day, Aisha told her students about the immense love that the Prophet ﷺ had for his daughter, Fatima.

"I have never seen anyone who embodied the demeanour, mannerisms and qualities of the Messenger of Allah ﷺ more than his daughter, Fatima, may Allah honour her," she said. "Whenever Fatima entered his home, the Prophet ﷺ would rise to greet her, take her hand, kiss her and seat her in his place. Likewise, when the Prophet ﷺ visited her, she would stand to welcome him, take his hand, kiss him and offer him her seat."

"O *Umm al-Mu'mineen*, what was the Messenger of Allah ﷺ like?" someone asked. Aisha smiled.

"Whenever Allah's Messenger ﷺ was given the choice between two matters, he would choose the easier of the two, if it was not sinful to do so. But if it was sinful to do so, he would not approach it," she said slowly and carefully. "Allah's Messenger ﷺ never took revenge on anybody for his own sake, but he only acted when Allah's laws were transgressed. In that case, he would avenge for Allah's sake."

At the end of the session, the students dispersed. But Aisha sensed that someone had remained behind the curtain. It was a young man. Clearing his throat, he spoke. "O Mother of the Believers, I am Abu Salamah," he said, "the son of Abdurrahman bin Awf."

Aisha's eyes widened as she realised who he was. "Your father accompanied the Mothers of the Believers on Hajj all those years ago," she reminisced. "How can I help you?"

"O Mother of the Believers, Urwah is better off than us!" Abdurrahman continued.

"How so?" Aisha inquired.

"Well, he, being your nephew, can visit you whenever he likes." Aisha's heart melted upon hearing the eagerness of the young student in her presence.

"There was no one closer to my family after the Prophet ﷺ than your father," Aisha said. "Do you know that once the Messenger of Allah ﷺ said to us, 'Only a truthful and pious person will be kind to you, the Mothers of the Believers'. Your father took us for the Hajj. He was truly a good man."

Then Aisha continued, "Look, whenever you like, you can sit outside my curtain and ask me whatever you want." Abdurrahman left the class that day beaming.

Her students' eagerness to learn soon helped to lift Aisha's spirits. Life in Madinah became so tranquil that the horrors of Basra seemed to fade into a distant memory, at least for now.

CHAPTER 38
The School of Aisha

Muhammad bin Abu Bakr was dead. Aisha wept softly for her younger brother. Surrounded by family, she picked up her baby nephew, Qasim, the son of Muhammad, and looked into his clear, dark eyes. He was a beautiful child, his plump cheeks nuzzling into her lap. As she wept, she reflected on how blissfully carefree he was, unaware of the dreadful news of his own father's demise.

After the Incident of the Camel, Caliph Ali faced a new challenge with Mu'awiyah. Overcome with anger and grief over his cousin Uthman's murder, Mu'awiyah believed that some murderers were hiding among Ali's followers and that he couldn't rest until they were brought to account. That quest for justice sparked clashes against the Caliph Ali's army, which endangered the unity of the Ummah.

When her brother Muhammad had travelled to Egypt as the new governor for that region, he got caught up in the ongoing rebellion against the caliph, led by Mu'awiyah's generals. Tragically, poor Muhammad was brutally killed by a ruthless soldier from Mu'awiyah's army. It was all so heartbreaking.

Aisha lifted her hands in supplication for her brother and prayed for peace. She prayed for the Ummah, just as Rasulullah ﷺ would have done. Seeing her nephew, Qasim, lying so peacefully in his mother's lap, Aisha decided she would help nurture him in her own home and make him her own student.

Urwah was orphaned; Aisha bint Talha - orphaned; and now Qasim - orphaned. Aisha saw in their beautiful faces the powerful potential that she had once had as a young student growing up in a house of knowledge. She would raise these nephews and nieces of hers with the greatest gift she could give them - sacred knowledge of the Quran and Sunnah. She would nurture them to be the most knowledgeable men and women of Madinah. 38 years had passed since the Hijrah. Aisha was over 40 years old now and she knew there was no time to lose.

More than 800 miles away from Madinah, in the city of Kufa in Iraq, the great Companion, Abu Musa al-Ash'ari was sitting with his students, narrating hadiths and telling them about life in Madinah. His students listened intently as he spoke.

"There was never a hadith the Companions of the Prophet ﷺ found difficult to understand," he began telling them, "except that when we asked Aisha, we found she had knowledge about it!" The students, many of whom had never set foot outside Kufa, were impressed and resolved to travel to Madinah to seek knowledge from *Umm al-Mu'mineen*.

Students flocked to Aisha, some who had travelled from distant lands, others who were right there in Madinah. Aisha especially doted on her younger students, just as a mother does upon her children. Urwah was so close to his aunt he could finish her sentences. He would sometimes lead Aisha in prayer, or sit and recite to her. She was, after all, one of the most knowledgeable people about the Quran. Whenever Urwah recited the verses that addressed the Mothers of the Believers, Aisha would ask him to stop. Then her eyes would well up and she'd weep and weep until her headscarf was soaked.

Aisha bint Talha was Aisha's orphaned niece and the daughter of Talha and Aisha's sister, Umm Kulthum. Aisha bint Talha's father, like Urwah's father, had been martyred during the Incident of the Camel. She was growing into a confident young lady with a strikingly pretty face, which drew the attention of the finest suitors in Arabia.

Little Qasim was but a lad and would lean on his aunt's crossed legs as she taught. He listened intently to every word, and Aisha would turn to him once in a while to make sure he understood what she was teaching.

Then there was Amrah bint Abdurrahman, a conscientious little girl who diligently lapped up everything she could from her teacher, Aisha. She had a sharp memory and made sure she understood Aisha's teachings thoroughly, by listening carefully and asking as many questions as she could. She was responsible for writing Aisha's letters.

Once Aisha was explaining to her students what had happened all those years ago during the incident of the slander. Someone in her presence criticised Hassan bin Thabit, the poet, for being one of those who'd fallen into spreading the rumours.

"No. You mustn't criticise him," Aisha insisted. "Don't you know he was the one who would defend the Prophet ﷺ from his enemies when they insulted him? He is the one who composed the verses:

'I give up my father and his father and my own honour,
To shield Muhammad's honour from you!'

Aisha's students understood Hassan had, of course, repented and made amends, and he had served the Prophet ﷺ in a way that they could never do. It was not right for them to criticise this great Companion of the Prophet ﷺ.

All the students learned good manners just by being with Aisha. No question was off-limits in her class. If someone made a mistake, Aisha would quickly point it out, but she always did so kindly, helping them understand.

Sometimes Aisha would walk with her students to run any errands she needed to in Madinah. They might pass by women who were exposing their beauty and wearing all manner of adornments in public. Aisha would be visibly upset. "If the Messenger of Allah saw the current state of women, he would stop them from coming to the masjid!" she remarked.

She advised the women not to focus too much on their looks or show off in public. "A woman who believes in Surah an-Nur cannot dress like this," she would say. These clothes didn't reflect the proper way believing women were commanded to dress when leaving their homes. If they ignored these guidelines, they would only earn sins.

Aisha reminded them of the reaction of the Ansari women when the hijab was revealed. "The women of Quraysh are good," she said, "but by Allah, I have never seen better women than the women of the Ansar - or any who believed the Book of Allah more strongly, or had more faith in the Revelation. When Surah an-Nur was revealed, saying: *'and to draw their head coverings all over their bodies'*, their menfolk came to them and recited to them what had been revealed. There was not a woman amongst them who did not go to get some cloth and return the following morning for prayer, wrapped up."

Aisha's students were amazed at how eager the women of Ansar had been to obey Allah's command without hesitation.

Just when Aisha thought the problem in the Ummah could not get any worse, she was informed that a faction of troublemakers from the town of Harura had killed Ali. Ali's death deeply affected her and everyone could sense the anger in her demeanour as they recounted the story of his demise to her.

"These atrocious people," Aisha lamented. "How harsh they are in their treatment of the Companions. Allah commands in the Quran that people should ask for His mercy and pray for the Companions. Instead, they hurled vulgarities and harmed them!"

With the assassination of Ali, the Ummah was once again in danger of plunging into chaos. People turned to Hasan, the son of Ali and Fatima and the grandson of the Prophet ﷺ, to lead them. Hasan was a wise young man, and wished for peace and unity, so he agreed to allow Mu'awiyah to become caliph, since he was the governor with the greatest influence and military might.

As for Aisha, she had already decided years ago to steer clear of all the political strife that the Ummah was experiencing. It had already brought her much pain and caused too much destruction.

During Hajj season, three sons of az-Zubayr sat together by the well of Zamzam, each wrapped in their two white sheets, their brown skin glistening in the sunlight. The majestic Ka'bah was right in front of them and the sky above was azure blue. The crowds of pilgrims had subsided for a moment, giving them a chance to rest and reminisce. Urwah, who was the middle-most brother, fetched a container of Zamzam for Abdullah, who was many years his senior. The youngest of them was their half-brother, Mus'ab, who had a different mother. Urwah's eyes twinkled when he noticed Ibn Umar approaching, and his cheeks broke out into a wide grin as he gestured to him to come sit with them for a while.

What a great blessing, Urwah marvelled, *to be sitting near the Ka'bah with these brothers, two of whom were Companions of the Prophet ﷺ.* His eyes widened and his fellow pilgrims could tell that a question was coming.

"Make a wish!" Urwah said, trying to capture the moment. "What do you desire that Allah bless you with?"

"I wish to be the caliph one day," said Abdullah.

Mus'ab gazed down at the ground for a while before raising his chin to reply. "I wish to be Governor of Iraq and to marry both your cousin, Aisha bint Talha, and the Prophet's ﷺ great granddaughter, Sukaynah bint Hussain."

"And you?" Urwah asked Ibn Umar.

"I wish to be forgiven by Allah," Ibn Umar replied.

They all nodded with approval before turning to Urwah to hear his response.

"As for me," Urwah said, thinking of his aunt Aisha and the great teachers he had left behind in Madinah, "I wish to be a scholar of Islam, from whom people take sacred knowledge."

Mus'ab placed a supportive hand on his brother's shoulder and squeezed. "May each of us be granted our wish!" he said, grinning.

"*Ameen*!" the others exclaimed.

In the 44th year after Hijrah, a messenger came to Aisha's door.

"O *Umm al-Mu'mineen*!" he said. "It is Umm Habibah; she lies ill in her bed."

Aisha understood right away the matter was serious. Upon entering her co-wife's quarters, Umm Habibah's grace struck her, even in her frail state. What a beautiful noblewoman she was - the daughter of Abu Sufyan, no less. Sister of the caliph Mu'awiyah. Today her eyes were sunken, for the Angel of Death was nearby.

Aisha came to Umm Habibah's side and prayed for her. Umm Habibah swallowed, mustering up the energy to speak. Tugging on Aisha's arm, she pleaded with her.

"O Aisha, there has been between us what usually happens between co-wives. May Allah forgive me and you for whatever happened of that nature." Aisha nodded, accepting her co-wife's words. By then, three of the Prophet's ﷺ wives had already passed away: Zaynab bint Khuzaymah during his lifetime, and Zaynab bint Jahsh and Mariyah after his passing.

"May Allah forgive you," Aisha said, "and pardon you for all of that, granting you freedom from it."

Umm Habibah closed her eyes, breathing a sigh of relief.

"You have made me happy," Umm Habibah said, opening her eyes as tears welled within them. "May Allah make you happy." She then sent for Umm Salamah to seek her forgiveness as well.

With the passing of Umm Habibah, only seven of the Mothers of the Believers remained.

When Urwah returned to Madinah from Hajj, he made sure to learn all he could from his aunt Aisha, for she was a fountain of knowledge that kept flowing and could never quench his thirst.

One day, he said to Aisha, "O my mother, I'm not surprised by your deep understanding of *fiqh* – Islamic law; after all, you are the wife of the Prophet of Allah and the daughter of Abu Bakr. Nor am I surprised by your knowledge of poetry and the history of people's lineages, since you are Abu Bakr's daughter, and he was the most knowledgeable of men in genealogy. But I am amazed by your knowledge of medicine. How did you come to learn so much about it?"

"O Urwah," Aisha said, gently tapping him on the shoulder. "The Messenger of Allah got sick near the end of his life, and people from all over Arabia came to visit him and would suggest different treatments. I used to prepare and give him those treatments, and that's how I learned."

Urwah's eyes widened in admiration. *My aunt's willingness to learn never ceases to amaze me*, he thought.

CHAPTER 39
Matriarch of Madinah

Groups of travellers were always entering and leaving Madinah. They would come to visit the Prophet's ﷺ masjid and, in doing so, would take some time out to visit the Mother of the Believers, Aisha, to ask her questions, or find out about medicinal remedies she had learned. Others came to listen to her stories about life with Rasulullah ﷺ.

At times, she would narrate *hadiths* - traditions about what the Prophet ﷺ said, did, or approved of. At other times, she would explain verses of Quran, knowing when they were revealed, why they were revealed, and how they could be applied in daily life. Aisha was always ready to answer their questions with the knowledge she had.

One day, a delegation from Egypt came to visit Aisha and inquire about something. One of the men in the delegation greeted her from behind the curtain.

Aisha still lived in her house. Although there was little space left, she could teach from her room from behind a curtain and the *hujrah* - the courtyard - could hold students too. It was her mission now, to convey all she had learned of the 'Book and Wisdom' - the Quran and Sunnah of the Prophet ﷺ to the Muslims. Soon, the Companions, who had lived and sat and walked with the Prophet ﷺ would be gone and there would be no one left on Earth who had even heard his voice.

"Where have you come from?" she asked the head of the delegation.

"I am from Egypt," the man replied. Aisha paused when she heard this. The wound of her brother's death at the hands of the Egyptian governor was still raw.

"What was the behaviour of your governor towards you in this recent war of yours?" she enquired.

"We experienced nothing bad from him," the man responded. "If one of our camels died, he would give us another camel. If any of us lost his slave, he would give him another slave. If anybody was in need of the basic necessities of life, he would provide them all."

Aisha was impressed.

"The way this man treated my brother, Muhammad bin Abi Bakr, does not prevent me from telling you what I heard from the Messenger of Allah," she said. "He said in this house of mine, 'O Allah, if a governor of my people is hard upon them, then You too, be hard upon him. But if he is kind to them, You be kind to him, too!'"

Despite her personal sorrow, Aisha knew people were not perfect and that it was important to be fair to them and faithfully convey all that she had learned. Allah had blessed her to have been the closest person to Rasulullah ﷺ. All that she had observed, all that she had asked, all that she knew, she would now pass on to the next generation.

There had been times when Aisha felt she must correct other Companions if she had some expertise about a matter that perhaps they did not.

"Is it true, as Ibn Umar says," Aisha heard her students discussing one day, "if a man kisses his wife, then his *wudu* is broken?"

"You mean he'd need to make a fresh *wudu* again before the next prayer?" someone else said.

Aisha's ears perked up at this.

"Allah have mercy on Ibn Umar," she said, "that is not correct!"

The handsome young man sitting closest to her was Urwah. His eyes brightened and the daylight shone on his face, revealing a finely kept beard and sparkling smile. He knew what his aunt would say next, as he had asked her about this before.

"The Messenger of Allah," the lady continued, "used to kiss one of his wives and go for the daily prayers without making *wudu* again."

"*Ahem*!" said Urwah playfully. "I wonder, was it you he would kiss?"

A smile flowered across Aisha's face and she looked away, blushing. Her nephews chuckled as, one after another, they took permission to leave for the masjid.

Another such occasion was when she corrected Abu Hurayrah, well known for narrating many sayings of the Prophet ﷺ. He had dedicated himself to staying in the masjid, listening and learning from the Prophet ﷺ when he was alive.

One day, Aisha came to hear that Abu Hurayrah was teaching people that a person's *salah* is void if a woman or a dog or a donkey passed in front of them.

Aisha was aghast. "May Allah have mercy on Abu Hurayrah. Is he likening us to dogs and donkeys in our effect upon the prayer?" Then she explained her reasoning through what she, as a woman, had personally experienced with the Messenger of Allah ﷺ. "My room was so small that my bed lay in front of Rasulullah's prayer mat. He stood in prayer and I lay stretched in bed, my feet dangling over the prayer mat. When he wanted to make *sajdah*, he would gently tap my feet and I pulled them back. Then I stretched them out again. Sometimes necessity drove me to pass in front of him as he stood in prayer."

Of course, Abu Hurayrah was not comparing women unfavourably. He was merely conveying a teaching, as he had understood it, about things that nullify the prayer. In fact, he valued the clarification from *Umm al-Mu'mineen* Aisha immensely.

Aisha was undoubtedly the matriarch of Madinah, just as the other Mothers of the Believers were in their own ways. She was always seeking the best for its people, like a mother wanting only good for her children. She kept a watchful eye on those who guided the community. One day, a young and zealous Imam, known for his long, ornate speeches, caught her attention. Concerned for the well-being of the people, she called him to speak to her.

The Imam, knowing her wisdom and stature, approached respectfully, standing behind the curtain as they exchanged greetings.

"Promise me three things, or I will be hard on you," Aisha said, getting straight to the point.

"What are the things, Mother of the Believers?" the Imam asked.

"You must be brief and direct in whatever you say in your speeches. Don't use this fancy language," she continued. "The Messenger of Allah and his Companions didn't do this."

The Imam looked surprised but listened carefully.

"You should give only one sermon a week," Aisha continued. "That is more than enough. If you are eager, then two and at most three. Don't tire people such that they turn away from the Book of Allah! Don't inflict long speeches on people. Give a speech when people really want one."

The Imam nodded sheepishly. "Yes, O Mother of the Believers. I will do as you advise."

One day when *Umm al-Mu'mineen* began teaching her students, she became speechless, deep in thought. She reflected on her blessed life, her eyes glistening. A student asked about her thoughts and her gratitude came pouring out.

"I was preferred over the wives of the Prophet in 10 ways," she said, "and I don't say this to boast."

"What are they, O *Umm al-Mu'mineen*?" asked her student.

"The Prophet did not marry any previously unmarried woman, except me. He didn't marry any woman whose parents were both Muhajirun, except me. Allah Almighty revealed my innocence from above the Heavens. The Angel Jibreel brought my image from Heaven embroidered with silk and said: 'Marry her, she is your wife'. The Prophet and I used to bathe ourselves from the same container and he did not do that with any of his other wives. The revelation would come down to him while he was with me, and it did not come down when he was with any of his other wives. He would pray while I was lying across his path, and he did not do this with any of his other wives. Allah took his soul while he was resting against my chest. He died on the night when it was my turn for him to stay with me, and he was buried in my room."

By this time, a number of the other Mothers of the Believers had passed away. Hafsah, Aisha's close friend and confidante, Maymunah, and Safiyyah had all left this worldly life. Then Sawdah also passed away. In her generosity, Sawdah had left her house to Aisha. Aisha was deeply grateful for this thoughtful gesture, as her own modest home barely had enough space for anything beyond sleeping. Sawdah's kindness was a reminder of the bonds they shared, and with her passing only three of the Mothers of the Believers remained.

Ever since his special birth in Quba many years ago, during the perilous journey from Madinah, Abdullah bin az-Zubayr had been Aisha's favourite nephew. She lavished him with love and affection.

Whenever Aisha received any gifts or her stipend from the caliph, she would simply instruct her servants to give it away. There were always those who were less well-off and, she wanted to follow in the footsteps of her beloved husband who had deliberately given up the luxuries of this world, hoping for them only in the Hereafter.

Abdullah once said about his aunt and his mother, "I have not seen anyone more generous than Aisha and Asma, though their generosity was different. Aisha would gather things, and after they had accumulated, she would share them. As for Asma, she would not leave anything for tomorrow."

When Abdullah heard about just how much his aunt would give away, he was worried about her. He believed his aunt should retain more of her gifts to meet her household needs. "Our beloved mother, Aisha, must stop doing this with her wealth or I'll have to force her to stop!" Abdullah remarked one day.

When Aisha heard that Abdullah had said this, she got rather angry. She was tired of people constantly telling her not to give so much to charity. Did they not know that it was Rasulullah ﷺ who had taught her not to be attached to the possessions of this world? Was Abdullah trying to stop her from doing good? He should know better!

"Did he really say this?" she exclaimed. "Will he prevent me from giving charity? I vow that I will not speak to him again!" she declared.

Oh dear, thought Abdullah, rubbing his forehead with worry. He had heard that his aunt was upset with him, and he knew how headstrong she was. When his aunt, Aisha, made an oath, she certainly kept it. *Perhaps I should give her some time to cool off. I mean, how serious could she really be?*

CHAPTER 40
Adviser to the Caliph

"They're turning us into a kingdom!" people began to whisper.

"Forcing people to pledge allegiance to their heirs!" others observed in agreement.

"Look at the soldiers lining the streets of Madinah!"

Abdurrahman bin Abi Bakr was making his way to the masjid with his neighbours when he noticed the military presence near the masjid. Under the caliphate of Mu'awiyah, things had changed so much. Still, there was at last some semblance of peace in Muslim lands.

Now Marwan bin al-Hakam was Governor of Madinah, and he lived in a grand old mansion with soldiers at the gate. He happened to be a cousin to the deceased Caliph Uthman, as well as to the new caliph, Mu'awiyah.

Today, Marwan had a swagger in his walk and was in a good mood. And why should he not be? He was Governor of Madinah, the Enlightened City. It was a beautiful day and Marwan was due to give an important speech in the Prophet's ﷺ masjid. Dressed in fine robes, he stood up straight with his shoulders back and chest out, as people gathered to listen.

Abdurrahman bin Abi Bakr entered the masjid quietly and sat down in his usual spot. As he examined the proceedings, he noted Marwan's decadent robes, his thin kohl-lined eyes and prominent dark eyebrows set on his large forehead. He had jewels on his fingers and an ornate belt around his waist. Abdurrahman was unimpressed. Before long, the people settled down and Marwan stood up grinning widely, ready to speak.

"O Muslims," Marwan began, rubbing his hands together and eyeing each person in the front row like an overexcited prince, sizing up his subjects at his coronation. "It is the wish of our dear caliph, before his passing away, that people pledge the oath of allegiance to his dear son, Yazid," he explained. The audience shuffled uncomfortably. Marwan continued to smile broadly, deaf to their discomfort.

"Now, this is, of course, perfectly in line with what the caliphs before Mu'awiyah would do," he said. "In fact, it is in the tradition, the *sunnah*, of Abu Bakr and Umar themselves! Did they not indicate their successors before they passed?"

Upon hearing his father's name, Abdurrahman was incensed and could no longer contain himself. He leapt to his feet. "No! No, it is not the sunnah of Abu Bakr and Umar!" he called out, pointing his finger toward Marwan. "It is, in fact, the 'sunnah' of Heraclius and Caesar!"

Heraclius was the Emperor of the Byzantine Empire, and Caesar ruled over Rome. Both maintained hereditary power within their families. The caliph was not meant to be a king. Abdurrahman and others feared that leadership in the Ummah might be passed down from father to son, turning it into a monarchy. While Abu Bakr and Umar had also named their successors before passing, they did so based on merit rather than family ties. The Caliph Mu'awiyah had another perspective. After years of conflict within the Ummah, Mu'awiyah sought to appoint his son as his successor to avoid further division.

Hearing the interruption from Abdurrahman, the congregation stirred. Marwan flushed red with rage. He shot a piercing side-glance at his soldiers, who looked unsure what to do. "Don't just stand there!" Marwan hollered. "Arrest him!"

Abdurrahman leapt through the rows, climbing over the heads of the congregation and falling through the gaps as quickly as he could. Then, as quick as a flash, he disappeared through the door that led to his sister's *hujrah*. Before Marwan's men could even know what was happening, Abdurrahman had slipped into Aisha's house and under her curtain.

Marwan stood there flummoxed; his men froze with confusion. They were not about to enter the home of the Mother of the Believers and breach its sanctity.
Marwan's men surrounded Aisha's house, waiting for Abdurrahman to give himself up. But it was no use. His sister had granted him safe refuge in her home. Marwan called impatiently for Abdurrahman.

"Hand yourself over!" he yelled hopelessly, his dark kohl-lined eyes darting around, trying to save face. The Madinans just stood with their arms folded, staring at Marwan. They certainly didn't want the Ummah to become a kingdom, with one caliph crowning his son as his successor, but they were also tired of conflict.

Marwan, realising that he had no way of reaching Abdurrahman, grew crimson with embarrassment.

"Aren't you, Abdurrahman, the wretched son?" he spat out in his desperation. "Disrespectful to his parents, about whom Allah revealed verses of rebuke in the Quran!"

Aisha could not let the insult go unchallenged. "No, by Allah!" she responded firmly. "Allah revealed nothing about us in the Quran except the truth of my innocence."

A flabbergasted Marwan recoiled awkwardly and shuffled away with his men. He knew better than to risk a sharp rebuke from Aisha, the Mother of the Believers.

In Makkah, Mu'awiyah had acquired properties and initiated numerous changes across the sacred city. The streets were alive with the sounds of construction - new structures rising and the landscape evolving under the desert sun. News of these activities soon reached the Prophet's ﷺ widow, Aisha, stirring concern within her. Were these developments truly for the Muslim Ummah, or were they a show of worldly ambition?

From her home in Makkah, where she occasionally journeyed, Aisha summoned Mu'awiyah, concerned about the rapid changes she had witnessed in the city. Mu'awiyah, ever-respectful of her stature, responded quickly to her call. Dhakwan, her trusted servant, stood at the door and welcomed the caliph inside upon his arrival.

From behind her curtain, Aisha addressed Mu'awiyah, her voice calmly demanding answers. "Are you the one who has turned Makkah into large buildings and palaces, though Allah, the Most High, gave it equally to all Muslims?"

Mu'awiyah, who was mindful of her esteemed position as the Mother of the Believers, answered humbly. "O Mother of the Believers, the people of Makkah are poor and lack shelter from the sun and rain. I call upon you to bear witness that everything I've built is given to them as charity."

Others present affirmed his statement, and Aisha's concerns softened. She soon learned that the new projects included wells for drinking water, continuous lighting for the Ka'bah, and other vital improvements to the city. Reassured, she understood Mu'awiyah intended his efforts for the people's well-being, not his own.

Times had changed, and with them had changed the stance of many of the Companions towards the caliphs. After all the strife of the previous years, peace was much dearer to them than worldly leadership tainted by bloodshed. So, although Aisha didn't agree with everything the caliph did, she would advise him privately, to prevent disorder in the Ummah.

Sometimes, Caliph Mu'awiyah would send his messenger to Madinah to ask Aisha for her *fiqh* opinions on different matters. As head of state, he faced many complex issues.

Letters and gifts from across the Muslim lands arrived at Aisha's home, containing questions and requests. She would instruct Amrah, dictating responses and occasionally sending gifts too. Her students were always on hand to assist.

One day, a delegation came from Damascus. It was Mu'awiyah's men, with a trunk full of gifts for Aisha. The trunk was overflowing with luxurious fabrics and beautiful dresses, jewellery and other trinkets. To their surprise, Aisha burst into tears when she saw these material things.

"The Messenger of Allah never touched any of this, nor owned anything like it," she remarked, her voice quavering through the tears. Accompanying the trunk of trinkets was a short letter from Mu'awiyah addressed to her. It was remarkably forthright:

"Peace be upon you. Please give me advice, and make it short," it read.

The messengers returned that afternoon and found Aisha dictating a letter. Her student, Amrah, sat with her ink pen, engrossed in writing. When she had finished, Amrah looked up from her scroll, rolled up the letter, and handed it through the curtain to the messengers.

It read:

"Assalamu alaykum.
A brief advice to the caliph. I have heard the Messenger of Allah ﷺ saying: 'Whoever seeks the pleasure of Allah, even though it displeases the people, Allah will protect him from the people's malice. But whoever pleases people by earning Allah's displeasure, then Allah will leave him to the mercy of the people!'
Peace be upon you, too."

By the evening, not one penny remained in Aisha's house. She ordered her servant to distribute all the gifts she had received.

When Caliph Mu'awiyah eventually visited Madinah, he sought an audience with Aisha. She granted him permission to meet her. He entered the room, standing behind the curtain, his shoulders hunched over and his gaze downward.

"O Mu'awiyah," Aisha said, rebuking the caliph for the actions of his men. "Where has the gentleness and magnanimity of Abu Sufyan, your father, gone? Where is it and where are you in comparison?"

Mu'awiyah, standing behind the curtain, loosened his collar. He looked forward to his meetings with Aisha. But he didn't much enjoy her tellings-off.

"O Mother of the Believers, your nephew, brother and others refuse to pledge allegiance to my son," Mu'awiyah complained. "I am only insisting on a successor to prevent bloodshed after me."

"O Mu'awiyah!" Aisha asserted. "I only press you to do one thing. Do not force these gentlemen against their will!"

Mu'awiyah sighed, shrugging his shoulders.

CHAPTER 41
A Nephew Reunited

Abdullah bin az-Zubayr paced around with his hands on his hips, unable to rest. His aunt, Aisha, hadn't spoken to him in a long time. It seems she was sticking to that oath she had made.

She must be regretting her words but unsure how to escape her vow, he thought. *She can't really still be angry with me, can she? Perhaps I did cross a line and hurt her feelings.*

Either way, he felt wretched and miserable. He sighed and in desperation headed out to meet two of the Prophet's ﷺ maternal relatives from the Banu Zuhrah tribe.

"Please," he implored, his eyes sullen but hopeful. "Help me to make amends with my aunt, Aisha. I cannot bear this any longer! I was the most devoted person to my aunt and was the most beloved person to her after Rasulullah and my grandfather, Abu Bakr."

"I think we can help you," the elders reassured him sympathetically, and so they began hatching a plan.

Abdullah really hoped that the plan would work. With his two uncles on either side, he headed towards his aunt, Aisha's house. He held his tongue in deathly silence as they waited outside her door.

"Assalamu alaykum, O *Umm al-Mu'mineen*," the two elderly men called. "May Allah's mercy and blessings be upon you! May we come in?"

Abdullah stood by their side with bated breath, afraid that his aunt would detect him. He swallowed hard.

"Yes, you may enter," Aisha said, recognising the voices of the elders.

"*All* of us?" the elders asked, looking at each other from the sides of their eyes and trying to keep a straight face.

"Indeed, all of you may enter," Aisha replied.

She could hear them shuffling through the door and stopping behind the curtain that separated her from them, as the men usually did.

Suddenly, as quick as a flash, Abdullah slipped through the curtain and gave his startled aunt a big bear hug.

Realising who it was, Aisha put her face in her hands and burst into tears, allowing him to embrace her tightly.

"O my dear aunt! How beloved you are to me," Abdullah said, holding her tightly, pleading for her forgiveness.

"But what of my vow?" Aisha cried, wishing she had never made it, knowing she ought not have. She knew how important it was to keep ties with her relatives - the Prophet ﷺ had taught them that turning away from family was never pleasing to Allah. But in a moment of upset, she had vowed not to speak to her nephew, and the burden of it had weighed heavily on her heart ever since.

"Do not worry about your vow at all!" Abdullah said, shaking with laughter. "I will send you 10 slaves to free so that you can absolve yourself of that vow!"

And he did.

CHAPTER 42
The End of an Era

The sunlight streamed in through the small window in Aisha's room, bathing her face in its golden warmth. It flashed brilliantly, illuminating every inch of her bed as the familiar clatter and soulful chatter of the dawn crescendoed into day. The striped curtain was gracefully drawn to the side, and there, amidst the soft glow, lay Aisha. Now around 65 years old, her hair, silver and soft, showed her age, and she lay breathing with clear discomfort. Despite her suffering, her spirit remained unshaken as she whispered *istighfar* and her lips moved with remembrance of Allah in the form of *dhikr*; *"La ilaha illallah,* there is nothing worthy of worship except Allah."

Moments later, Aisha blinked, startled to find her nephews sitting around her bed having a quiet discussion.

"A life richly lived, dear aunt," one nephew remarked, his voice thick with emotion, yet brimming with an undeniable pride. Aisha's eyes, deep wells of wisdom and experience, fluttered shut momentarily. While she appreciated the warmth of their words, she understood deep down that the true measure of her life lay in whether she had fulfilled her covenant with Allah. That eternal truth had been the guiding compass for all her actions and thoughts.

A flood of memories swirled around her, each one tied to her unwavering devotion to the Messenger of Allah ﷺ. She recalled the days she had stood by his side as his solace and joy. She remembered the bridge of understanding she had built with Ali. Bonds once strained had been tenderly mended. Forgiveness had been their shared consolation. Aisha had tried to ensure that every nugget of knowledge, each lesson about the Quran she had learned from the Messenger of Allah ﷺ, and all she had observed of his Sunnah, was passed down, like prized family jewellery, to her devoted pupils.

Knowing her pivotal role, Aisha explained the teachings of Islam to people with clarity and precision. She offered encouragement when hearts needed lifting and firm admonition when the situation called for it.

She knew the expanding Muslim community looked to her for wisdom, especially since the era of the Prophet's ﷺ

Companions was ending. Soon there would be no one left on Earth who had met the Messenger of Allah ﷺ.

But the rustling of life in Madinah reminded her that the world had thrived before her and would continue long after. She no longer carried its burdens; she had fulfilled her sacred duty. The responsibility of upholding Allah's teachings now rested safely on her students' capable shoulders. This gave Aisha the contentment she had been looking for ever since the passing of Rasulullah ﷺ. If Allah was pleased with her, she would have fulfilled her duty.

It was the 17th night of Ramadan, and Madinah was aglow with a deeper sense of tranquillity. Every direction echoed with the Quran's harmonious verses. Aisha listened to the hum of recitation around her.

Awash with glorious memories of days filled with light, nights of deep thought and moments of collective joy, she recognised each as a sign of Allah's endless generosity. How could she be anything but grateful?

"Let me find rest with my sisters in Baqi cemetery, not beside the Prophet, Abu Bakr, or Umar," Aisha said firmly.

Her nephews looked at each other with surprise. "But, our mother, your rightful place is beside Rasulullah and your father," one of them said gently.

Aisha frowned, motioning her hand as if to usher the idea away. "Then all of my repentance would come to nothing," she said. Her nephews fell silent as she continued. "Besides this, I would not like to be seen as better than I truly am."

Nodding with understanding, her nephews respected her wishes.

"When I have been shrouded and scented," she continued, instructing her nephews, "let Dhakwan lower me into my grave and level the earth over me. Then set him free."

"I seek forgiveness from Allah," she whispered again and again. And with a final prayer, Aisha, daughter of Abu Bakr closed her eyes, surrendering to the encircling peace, free at last from worldly fetters.

"O soul at peace, return to your Lord,
content and well-pleasing.
Join My faithful servants,
and enter into My Garden."
(Quran, 89:27-30)

CHAPTER 43
Madinah Mourns

"Umm Salamah!" rang the voices outside. The gentle silence of the Ramadan night was broken just as Umm Salamah was wrapping up her evening prayers. She looked out of her window and saw the sky cloaked in velvet darkness, its stars shimmering like silver sequins.

"What is it?" Umm Salamah enquired, wondering what had caused such commotion on an otherwise peaceful evening.

"It is your companion!" the people of Madinah cried, wiping their eyes and noses.

"It is Aisha!"

"She has journeyed to the Hereafter."

Umm Salamah's lips trembled. Tears welled in her eyes, blurring her vision as she realised she was now the last of the Prophet's ﷺ wives left. Juwairiyah had passed away two years ago, leaving only Aisha and Umm Salamah as the remaining Mothers of the Believers. They had all journeyed through the highs and lows of life together during the lifetime of the Messenger of Allah ﷺ. They'd witnessed Islam's message unfurl from the heart of Madinah to the furthest reaches - and they had become its teachers. After the Prophet's ﷺ passing, they held the torch of his Sunnah together, lighting the path for the Ummah.

"O Aisha, dear Aisha, may Allah shower His mercy upon her!" Umm Salamah lamented. "After her father, she held the most cherished place in the Prophet's heart."

In the masjid, as the Imam concluded the prayers, a voice broke the solemnity: "O servants of Allah! Our mother, Aisha, has returned to her Lord!" The air thickened with mournful gasps and rueful cries.

"Alas, alas, we have lost a great teacher!"

"She, who received special instruction from the Messenger of Allah, has departed from us!"

People, both young and old, spilled out onto the streets of Madinah as the news reached them. Aisha stood as the unique bond to the Messenger of Allah ﷺ for so many who had never had the privilege of meeting him.

"We have lost *habibatu habibillah*! We have lost the beloved of Allah's beloved!"

They understood that with the passing of Aisha, a window into the life of Rasulullah ﷺ had closed forever.

The people of Madinah, moved by the news, converged around the burial ground. They had not seen so many women gather outside except on Eid days. The pathways swelled with children, some with sandals, others barefoot, and even the frail and elderly made their way with determination. Those who were already in the masjid, joined those making their way towards the Baqi cemetery, keen to join the *janazah* prayer and pay homage to Aisha.

They lit a torch to guide Aisha's bier - the wooden stretcher that carried her shrouded body. Abu Hurayrah stepped forward, his silhouette illuminated by the flickering flame, ready to lead her funeral prayer. He was the greatest of the Prophet's ﷺ Companions still in Madinah.

"*Allahu Akbar*!" Abu Hurayrah declared, raising his hands - and thousands of hands rose with his.

The full moon hanging brightly in the inky blue-black sky was a clear reminder that half the month of Ramadan had gone. A group of fine, gallant men, including Aisha's devoted nephews, Urwah, Abdullah and Qasim, hoisted her bier onto their shoulders. The torch-flame's vibrant orange glow flickered intensely, illuminating the faces of the pallbearers and casting moving shadows on the sombre figures of the mourners.

They made their way inside the sacred grounds of Baqi. Beneath its soil lay seven of the Prophet's ﷺ wives: Sawdah, Hafsah, Umm Habibah, the two Zaynabs, Safiyyah and Juwayriyah. Now, in accordance with her final wish, Aisha would be laid beside them.

Nearing the hallowed burial site, they raised a tent over the grave, ensuring she was respected with the highest degree of privacy. Inside, they gently lowered her shrouded form into its final resting place as everyone watched on. Meanwhile, clusters of men and women converged around the burial ground, bearing silent tribute.

As dawn painted the horizon with hues of gold and muted lavender, a delicate mist enveloped Madinah, the city's majestic palm trees standing with a solemn stillness as silent witnesses to the grave loss.

Qasim bin Muhammad, bathed in the early morning light, stood amidst an eager crowd, recounting Aisha's unparalleled wisdom. Once a student in his aunt's lap, today he was one of the famous Seven Great Jurists of Madinah.

"I did not meet anyone as eloquent as my aunt, Aisha," he said to those who had gathered, "nor anyone more knowledgeable about Islamic theology than her. Not amongst men nor women."

As the news spread, scholars and leaders from distant lands began sharing their heartfelt eulogies. In the city of Kufa, the renowned sage, al-Ahnaf bin Qays remarked, "I have heard the speeches of Abu Bakr, Umar, Uthman and Ali, and the caliphs succeeding them, but I have not heard any speech more persuasive and magnificent from the mouth of any person than from the mouth of Aisha."

Scholars and students alike recalled that the Prophet ﷺ had once said of Aisha, "Many men reached perfection but none among the women reached perfection except Mary, the daughter of Imran, and Asiya, Pharaoh's wife. The superiority of Aisha over other women is like the superiority of *tharid* over other kinds of food."

Later, the fragrant courtyard of Urwah's mansion was alive with visitors. They listened intently while he reflected on his aunt, her words and teachings lingering in his thoughts.

"In all my years," he said, his smile bitter-sweet. "I've not encountered anyone with greater knowledge than my aunt Aisha in medicine, *fiqh* and poetry."

He told them how, with the passing of Khadijah, the Prophet ﷺ was deeply grief-stricken, and it was during that time that Allah had sent the Angel Jibreel in a dream to comfort him. Jibreel presented the Prophet ﷺ with an image of Aisha, which reassured him that marrying her would help ease his heartache.

"In these recent four years with *Umm al-Mu'mineen*," Urwah said, "I had realised that if she was to pass away, there isn't a single hadith in her vast repository of wisdom I am not familiar with. She had taught me them all."

Urwah stepped into his orchard as the visitors followed him, hanging on his every word. Gazing at a bunch of ripe dates, Urwah reminisced about times gone by, when he had accompanied his aunt daily and the world seemed full of the Companions of the Prophet ﷺ.

"My aunt, Aisha, may Allah be pleased with her, was so generous and lived so simply," Urwah said, tears coming to his eyes, "that she would give 70,000 coins in charity while her own clothes were covered in patches."

Urwah's mind drifted to that distant day in Makkah on Hajj, when he and his brothers had made wishes by the Ka'bah. How generous was Allah that all their wishes had come true! Mus'ab did indeed become Iraq's governor and had wedded both Aisha bint Talha and Sukaynah bint Hussain. Abdullah was on the path to becoming caliph. Urwah himself had risen in rank as a revered scholar and jurist of Madinah, drawing knowledge-seekers from across the Ummah. And as for Ibn Umar, they all hoped and expected that Allah would grant him his wish too and indeed forgive him.

Aisha's teachings had shaped Urwah's vision, and he felt a renewed commitment to her legacy. He would continue to teach the Sunnah of the Messenger ﷺ and to heed her advice for as long as he lived. His aunt, Aisha, had taught him that to live a life pleasing to Allah was a person's highest obligation.

"Masha Allah," Urwah said, a faint smile upon his face as he thought about her. He would continue to open up his orchard to the poor and needy, just as his aunt had taught him. And as he admired his blossoming garden, he recited the words of Surah al-Kahf:

"This is what Allah has willed!
There is no power except with Allah!"
(Quran, 18:39)

Urwah looked up at the sky and took a deep breath. 58 years had passed since the Hijrah. The unstoppable cycle of life and death, of generations departing and new generations arriving, was all part of Allah's perfect plan. And as he walked out of his home towards the masjid, the air around

Madinah felt different. Like an era had ended and the dawn of a new one had arrived, one without his aunt, Aisha.

And yet, Aisha's spirit lived on, for the knowledge she narrated, the lessons she taught and the stories she told were recorded and passed down by her students, first orally and then through the great books of hadith. Aisha's voice would echo beyond their generation, guiding souls with the teachings of Rasulullah ﷺ, until the end of time.

So, if you, dear reader, should ever want to hear from our mother, Aisha, you could open up one of the great books of hadith. She'll be right there, painting vivid pictures on the canvas of your mind, each brush-stroke teaching you how to think and sharing every extraordinary adventure in vibrant colours. And were you to do so, you would feel as though she was sitting right next to you, like a close friend or a loving aunt, and you would bask in the warmth of her smile, weep along with her tears, and relive every vivid detail of her life with Rasulullah ﷺ.

And should you, dear reader, ever wish to visit the house of our mother, Aisha, where she lived and taught, and send your greetings upon the Prophet ﷺ, Abu Bakr and Umar, who are laid to rest there, you need look no further than the magnificent green dome of the Prophet's ﷺ masjid in Madinah. For they lie right beneath it - in the house of the clever, the scholarly, the generous, the lively, the inimitable, the devoted, the maternal and the affectionate - daughter of *al-Siddiq*, wife of *al-Mustafa*, mother to us all: Aisha.

The Best Generation

The Companions of the Prophet ﷺ were the finest human beings in rank, after the Prophets. Allah describes them in the Quran thus:

"Allah is pleased with them,
and they are pleased with Him."
(Quran, 9:100)

These dedicated individuals played a pivotal role in preserving Islam for future generations. They were chosen by Allah to be the Prophet's ﷺ Companions and the best generation. Our Islamic teachings emphasise the importance of holding each of these Companions in high esteem and steering clear of negative opinions.

Through Aisha's story, the humanity of the Sahaba shines through and triumphs. They, like every human, had their struggles, but we know they navigated each challenge with integrity and the best of intentions. It is essential that we approach their stories with reverence and understanding, abstaining from speculation and negative interpretations.

As the Quran says:

"That was a community that has passed on.
What they earned belongs to them, and what you earn
belongs to you. And you will not be
answerable for their deeds."
(Quran, 2:141)

Key Figures

Abbad bin Bishr: A devout Companion of the Prophet ﷺ from the Ansar, known for his deep piety and courage in battle.

Abdullah bin Abdurrahman: Aisha's nephew and son of her brother, Abdurrahman. He stayed by her side during her final illness.

Abdurrahman bin Abi Bakr: Aisha's full brother, son of Abu Bakr and Umm Ruman. He embraced Islam later during the Madinan period.

Abdurrahman bin Awf: A wealthy and generous Companion of the Prophet Muhammad ﷺ, and one of The 10 Promised Paradise.

Abu Ayyub al-Ansari: The Companion who first hosted the Prophet Muhammad ﷺ in his home in Madinah. He participated in many conquests and is buried in modern-day Türkiye.

Abu Bakr as-Siddiq: Aisha's father, the first caliph of Islam, and the Prophet Muhammad's ﷺ closest Companion. He was known for his steadfast faith and leadership.

Abu Hurayrah: Companion of the Prophet ﷺ who narrated the most hadith. He led the funeral prayer of Aisha.

Abu Jahl: A Quraysh chieftain named Abul-Hakam, which means 'Father of Wisdom'. The Muslims referred to him as Abu Jahl, 'Father of Ignorance', because of his severe oppression of them.

Abu Musa al-Ash'ari: A Companion of the Prophet ﷺ known for his beautiful Quranic recitation and hadith narration. He served as Governor of Iraq during Umar's caliphate.

Abu Quhafah: Aisha's paternal grandfather and the father of Abu Bakr. He embraced Islam after the Conquest of Makkah.

Abu Rafi: A Companion of the Prophet ﷺ, he was a Coptic slave who embraced Islam and was entrusted with the security of female travellers. He accompanied Aisha's family during their Hijrah.

Abu Salamah bin Abdurrahman: A student of Aisha and the son of the Companion Abdurrahman bin Awf.

Abu Sufyan: A chieftain of Quraysh who later became a great Companion of the Prophet ﷺ and was the father of the Caliph Mu'awiyah.

Abdullah bin Abi Bakr: Aisha's half-brother, son of Abu Bakr and Qutailah bint Abdul Uzza.

Abdullah bin az-Zubayr: Aisha's nephew, who was born during her Hijrah. He was the son of her sister, Asma, and az-Zubayr bin al-Awwam.

Abdullah, the son of Ibn Salul: A righteous Companion, despite his father, Ibn Salul, being the leader of the Hypocrites. His full name was Abdullah bin Ubayy bin Salul.

Aisha bint Talha: Niece and student of Aisha. Daughter of Talha bin Ubaydillah, and Aisha's sister, Umm Kulthum. She married Mus'ab bin az-Zubayr.

Ali bin Abi Talib: The Prophet's ﷺ cousin, the first youth to embrace Islam, and husband of Fatima, the Prophet's ﷺ daughter. He was the fourth caliph of Islam and one of The 10 Promised Paradise.

Amr bin al-Aas: A Companion of the Prophet ﷺ, known for his role as the conqueror and Governor of Egypt.

Amrah bint Abdurrahman: A student and personal secretary of Aisha, who became a respected scholar of hadith in her own right.

Anas bin Malik: A Companion and Servant of the Prophet ﷺ. He participated in many of the early Muslim battles.

Asma bint Abi Bakr: Aisha's elder half-sister, daughter of Abu Bakr and Qutailah bint Abdul Uzza, known as *Dhat an-Nitaqayn* (the Lady with the Two Belts). Abdullah and Urwah were her sons.

Asma bint Umays: A Companion of the Prophet ﷺ, wife of Abu Bakr and later wife of Caliph Ali. She was the mother of Muhammad bin Abi Bakr.

Az-Zubayr bin al-Awwam: Aisha's brother-in-law, who was the Prophet's ﷺ cousin and husband of Asma bint Abi Bakr. His sons included Abdullah, Urwah and Mus'ab. Az-Zubayr was one of The 10 Promised Paradise.

Barirah: A servant of Aisha who assisted with cooking and food preparation.

Bilal bin Rabah: Companion of the Prophet Muhammad ﷺ and the first muezzin, Bilal was known for his beautiful voice and strong faith. Abu Bakr freed him from slavery.

Dhakwan: A slave boy of Aisha who used to lead her in prayers. She freed him upon her death.

Fatima: The daughter of the Prophet ﷺ and Khadijah. She was Aisha's stepdaughter and wife of Caliph Ali bin Abi Talib.

Habibah bint Kharijah: A wife of Abu Bakr and mother of his youngest daughter, Umm Kulthum.

Hala bint Khuwaylid: A sister of *Umm al-Mu'mineen*, Khadijah.

Hasan bin Ali: The grandson of the Prophet ﷺ who was briefly recognised as caliph after Ali. Hasan was respected for his role in promoting peace by standing down from power.

Hassan bin Thabit: A Companion and poet of the Prophet ﷺ.

Ibn ad-Daghnah: The chief of the Qara tribe.

Ibn Salul (full name Abdullah bin Ubayy bin Salul): Leader of the Hypocrites in Madinah.

Ibn Abbas (full name Abdullah bin Abbas): Cousin of the Prophet ﷺ and son of his uncle al-Abbas. He was a renowned scholar known as *al-Bahr* (the Ocean) for his extensive knowledge of the Quran.

Ibn Umar (full name Abdullah bin Umar): Scholar of Islam, son of Caliph Umar, and brother of the Prophet's ﷺ wife, Hafsah.

Ibn Urayqeet: A desert guide hired by the Prophet ﷺ and Abu Bakr during their Hijrah. His full name was Abdullah bin Urayqeet.

Jubayr bin Mut'im: Formerly engaged to Aisha before the engagement was broken off. He later embraced Islam.

Ka'b: Judge of Basra in Iraq, who joined Aisha's side during the Incident of the Camel.

Khawla bint Hakim: The woman who suggested to the Prophet ﷺ that he marry Aisha and conveyed the proposal to her family.

Marwan bin Hakam: Governor of Madinah during Mu'awiyah's reign and later became the eighth caliph.

Mistah bin Uthathah: A second cousin of Aisha, and son of Abu Bakr's cousin. He was a Companion of the Prophet ﷺ, a veteran of the Battle of Badr, and received financial support from Abu Bakr.

Mu'awiyah bin Abi Sufyan: Companion of the Prophet ﷺ, son of Qurayshi leader Abu Sufyan and Hind bint Utbah, cousin of Uthman, and the fifth caliph.

Muhammad bin Abi Bakr: He was considered a *tabi'i*, which means he was from the generation after the Prophet's ﷺ Companions. As the youngest half-brother of Aisha, he was just an infant when the Prophet ﷺ passed away. His mother was Asma bint Umays and he was raised by his stepfather, Caliph Ali, after Abu Bakr's death.

Mus'ab ibn az-Zubayr: A half-brother of Abdullah and Urwah bin az-Zubayr. Husband of Aisha's niece, Aisha bint Talha.

Mut'im bin Adi: A nobleman of Makkah. His son Jubayr was temporarily engaged to Aisha.

Na'ilah bint al-Furafisa: Wife of the Caliph Uthman, who was injured during his assassination.

Qasim bin Muhammad: Son of Aisha's brother, Muhammad bin Abi Bakr. He was a student of Aisha, who became one of the renowned Seven Jurists of Madinah.

Al-Qa'qa bin Amr: Military commander who served in the armies of the first four caliphs.

Sa'd bin Mu'adh: Ansari leader of the Aws tribe in Madinah.

Sa'd bin Ubadah: Ansari leader of the Khazraj tribe in Madinah, who provided a feast for Aisha's wedding day.

Safwan bin al-Mu'attal: Companion of the Prophet ﷺ and a skilled warrior who was wrongfully slandered by Ibn Salul.

Shaibah bin Uthman: Key-bearer of the Ka'bah, historically known for his clan's role in holding the Ka'bah keys since pre-Islamic times.

Talhah bin Ubaydillah: A close Companion of the Prophet ﷺ and one of The 10 Promised Paradise. He was married to Aisha's youngest sister, Umm Kulthum, and was the father of the renowned scholar, Aisha bint Talhah.

Umar bin al-Khattab: Companion of the Prophet ﷺ, the second caliph, father of Hafsah, the Prophet's ﷺ wife.

Umm Ayman (full name Barakah bint Tha'labah): The Prophet's ﷺ foster mother and wife of Zayd bin Harithah. She was the mother of Usama bin Zayd.

Umm Ayyub: Wife of Abu Ayyub al-Ansari.

Umm Dharrah: A later maid-servant of Aisha.

Umm Kulthum: The youngest sister of Aisha and daughter of Abu Bakr and Habibah bint Kharijah. She was married to Talhah bin Ubaydillah and was the mother of Aisha bint Talhah.

Umm Mistah: A cousin of Abu Bakr, daughter of his maternal aunt, and mother of Mistah bin Uthathah.

Umm Ruman: Mother of Aisha and Abdurrahman, and second wife of Abu Bakr.

Uqbah bin Abi Mu'ayt: A disbeliever from Makkah known for his violent attacks and strong opposition against the Prophet ﷺ and the Muslims.

Urwah bin az-Zubayr: Aisha's nephew and son of her sister, Asma. He was a student of Aisha who narrated many hadiths from her. He became one of the prominent Seven Jurists of Madinah.

Usama bin Zayd: Son of Zayd bin Harithah and Umm Ayman, who was like a grandson to the Prophet ﷺ.

Uthman bin Affan: The fourth caliph of Islam and twice the son-in-law of the Prophet ﷺ.

Zayd bin Arqam: A young Companion of the Prophet ﷺ who overheard and reported Ibn Salul's plotting.

Zayd bin Thabit: Companion and scribe of the Prophet ﷺ, renowned for his exceptional knowledge of the Quran and his pivotal role in compiling the sacred text.

Zayd bin Harithah: Companion of the Prophet ﷺ. A former slave gifted to the Prophet ﷺ by Khadijah, whom the Prophet ﷺ had adopted as a son.

Mothers of the Believers (Wives of the Prophet ﷺ)

Aisha: Daughter of Abu Bakr as-Siddiq and Umm Ruman.

Hafsah bint Umar: Daughter of Umar bin al-Khattab.

Juwayriyyah bint al-Harith: A noblewoman from the Banu Mustaliq tribe, she was captured in battle and later freed by the Prophet Muhammad ﷺ.

Khadijah bint Khuwaylid: The Prophet's ﷺ first wife and the mother of Fatima. She passed away before he married Aisha.

Maymunah bint al-Harith: From the Hilali tribe, her marriage to the Prophet ﷺ helped strengthen ties between various tribes in the community.

Mariyah al-Qibtiyyah: An Egyptian woman gifted to the Prophet ﷺ by the Christian Governor of Alexandria, later freed by him. She was a wife of Prophet Muhammad ﷺ and the mother of his son, Ibrahim, who died in childhood.

Safiyyah bint Huyay: A noblewoman from the Jewish tribe of Banu Nadir who embraced Islam and became a wife of the Prophet Muhammad ﷺ.

Sawdah bint Zam'ah: The second wife of the Prophet ﷺ whose marriage took place in Makkah.

Umm Habibah (Ramlah bint Abi Sufyan): The daughter of Abu Sufyan, a chieftain of Makkah, and the half-sister of Mu'awiyah.

Umm Salamah (Hind bint Abi Umayyah): She married the Prophet ﷺ after her husband died in the Battle of Uhud.

Zaynab bint Jahsh: Known for her deep faith and generosity, she was among the Prophet's ﷺ most charitable wives.

Zaynab bint Khuzaimah: She married the Prophet ﷺ after her previous husband died in battle. Zaynab passed away just eight months after their marriage, making her the second of his wives to die during his lifetime.

Glossary

Abyssinia: an ancient kingdom located in present-day Ethiopia and Eritrea, known for its Christian ruler who embraced Islam. It was a place of refuge for early Muslims fleeing persecution in Makkah.

As-Siddiq: an Arabic term that translates to 'the truthful' or 'the sincere'. It is a title given to Abu Bakr, one of the closest Companions of Prophet Muhammad ﷺ in Islam, known for his steadfastness in faith and his honesty.

Caliph: From the Arabic *khalifah*, meaning 'successor'. The leader of the Muslim community after the Prophet Muhammad ﷺ, also known as the Commander of the Faithful (*Amir al-Mu'mineen*).

Caravan: A group travelling together, often for trade, across deserts.

Duff: A round, hand-held drum made of wood and animal skin, used in Middle Eastern celebrations. Striking it produces a rhythmic sound and people often play it at festivals and special events.

Du'a: A personal supplication where a person calls on Allah, asking for help, seeking forgiveness, or sharing their wishes and thoughts.

Fiqh: The understanding and interpretation of Islamic law. *Fiqh* covers many topics, including prayer, fasting, charity, marriage and business dealings.

Fustat: A city of tents established by the Companion Amr bin al-Aas in Egypt after the Muslim conquest. It later grew into part of what is now modern-day Cairo.

Hadith: Recorded sayings, actions or approvals of Prophet Muhammad ﷺ, used as a source of guidance in Islamic law and practices.

Hawdaj: A covered seat for women on camels in Arabia.

Hijaz: A region in the modern-day western region of Saudi Arabia, home to the holy cities of Makkah and Madinah.

Hijrah: Means 'migration'. We usually mean by it the journey of Prophet Muhammad ﷺ from Makkah to Madinah in 622 CE. Many other Companions made this journey too.

Hypocrites: Also known as *'Munafiqun'*, are people who pretend to believe in Islam but secretly work against it. They say they are Muslims, but in their hearts, they do not truly have faith.

Istighfar: Saying *"Astaghfirullah,"* which means, "I seek forgiveness from Allah."

Jaddi: Means 'my grandfather' in Arabic.

Jilbab: A loose outer garment worn by Muslim women when they go out or are in the presence of non-*mahram* men, to cover their body, including the head and neck.

Kunya: A respectful nickname for adults or children, often using one's child's name or a characteristic one is known for e.g. Abu Yusuf for the father of Yusuf, or Umm al-Khayr meaning the Mother of Goodness.

Khimar: A headscarf worn by Muslim women.

Luban: Frankincense, a sweet-smelling resin from the Boswellia tree, used in incense, perfumes and traditional medicine.

Mahram: A close male relative a woman cannot marry, like her father, brother or son, and with whom she can travel or be in private.

Maqam Ibrahim: A special stone near the Ka'bah in Makkah. It has the footprints of Prophet Ibrahim on it, from when he helped build the Ka'bah.

Al-Masjid an-Nabawi: The Prophet Muhammad's ﷺ masjid in Madinah.

Mimbar: The platform in a masjid for giving sermons.

Mudd: A unit of measurement from Madinah, roughly equal to 0.75 to 1.0 litre, used for measuring food like grains, especially in Islamic practices like zakah (charity).

Muezzin: A person who performs the *adhan*, the call to prayer, chosen to serve at the masjid as a muezzin because of their good character and vocal skills.

Mus-haf: A written copy of the Quran.

Rawdah: A sacred area in Masjid al-Nabawi, between the Prophet Muhammad's ﷺ tomb and pulpit, described as a 'garden of Paradise'.

Sa': A traditional unit of measurement in Arabia, equivalent to about 2.5 to 3 litres, used for measuring larger quantities of food, such as grains or dates, now often used for giving in charity.

As-Sābiqūn al-Awwalūn: "The First and Foremost" - The earliest Muslims who accepted Islam and supported the Prophet ﷺ.

Salah: The ritual prayers, performed five times a day.

Seven Jurists of Madinah: A group of distinguished religious scholars during the second generation after Prophet Muhammad ﷺ: Sa'id bin al-Musayyib, Urwah bin al-Zubayr,

Qasim bin Muhammad bin Abi Bakr, Ubaydullah bin Abdullah bin Utbah bin Mas'ud, Kharija bin Zayd, Sulayman bin Yasar, and Abu Salamah bin Abdurrahman bin Awf. Many of them were close students of Aisha.

Shaykh: In Arabic, shaykh means an elderly man or a learned religious scholar or tribal leader.

Sunnah: The way of life and practices of Prophet Muhammad ﷺ. Also means 'tradition'.

Sahaba: The Companions of Prophet Muhammad ﷺ, the people who were Muslims and met or saw the Prophet ﷺ in person. They were his first followers and we hold them in the highest regard.

Tabi'i: A successor. Meaning a person from the generation after the *Sahaba*, who met or saw a Companion of the Prophet ﷺ.

Taqwa: means fear of Allah or God-consciousness.

Tayammum: Using clean soil or dust to purify when there is no water.

The 10 Promised Paradise: 10 early Muslims, including the four caliphs and prominent Companions of the Prophet ﷺ, who were guaranteed Paradise for their unwavering commitment to Islam: Abu Bakr as-Siddiq, Umar bin al-Khattab, Uthman bin Affan, Ali bin Abi Talib, Talhah bin Ubaydillah, az-Zubayr bin al-Awwam, Abdurrahman bin Awf, Sa'd bin Abi Waqqas, Sa'id bin Zayd and Abu Ubaydah al-Jarrah.

Ummah: The Ummah is the nation and family of people who follow Prophet Muhammad ﷺ. Every Muslim, from his time until the end of the world, belongs to his Ummah.

Yathrib: The old name for the city of Madinah.

Bibliography

English Books and Translations

Anas, Malik Ibn. *Al-Muwatta of Imam Malik*. Translated by Aisha Abdurrahman Bewley. 3rd edition. Bradford: Diwan Press, 2014.

Hamid, Abdulwahid. *Companions of the Prophet 1*, 2nd edition. London: MELS, 1998.

Hamid, Abdulwahid. *Companions of the Prophet 2*, 2nd edition. London: MELS, 1998.

Knight, Nuriddeen. *40 Hadith of 'Aisha*. Nuriddeen, 2018.

Mubarakpuri, Safi-ur-Rahman. *Ar-Raheeq Al-Makhtum (The Sealed Nectar): Biography of the Prophet*. Riyadh: Dar-us-Salam Publications, 2002.

Nadvi, Allamah Syed Sulaiman. *Hadhrat Ayesha Siddiqa: Her Life & Works*. Karachi: Darul Ishaat, 2010.

Resit Haylamaz. *Aisha: The Wife, the Companion, the Scholar.* New Jersey: Tughra Books, 2013.

Sa'd, Muhammad Ibn. *Kitab At-Tabaqat Al-Kabir Volume III: The Companions of Badr.* 1st Edition. London: Ta-Ha Publishers Ltd, 2013.

Sa'd, Muhammad Ibn. *Kitab At-Tabaqat Al-Kabir Volume VIII.* Translated by Aisha Bewley. London: Ta-Ha Publishers Ltd, 1995.

Sallabi, Muhammad al-. *The Biography of Abu Bakr As-Siddique.* Edited by Darussalam Publishers. Riyadh: Darussalam Publishers & Distributers, 2020.

Sallabi, Ali Muhammad. *The Biography of 'Ali Ibn Abi Talib.* 1st Edition. Riyadh: Darussalam, 2011.

Suyuti, Jalal ad-Din as-. *The History of the Khalifas Who Took the Right Way.* 2nd Revised edition. London: Ta-Ha Publishers Ltd, 2008.

Zahrani, Nasir Misfir al-. *The Prophet's Food and Drinks.* Al-Salam Endowments Foundation, 2021.

Nadwi, Mohammad Akram. *Al-Muhaddithat: The Women Scholars in Islam.* 2nd revised edition. Oxford: Interface Publications Ltd, 2013.

Arabic Books

Al-Bukhari, Muhammad ibn Ismail. *Saheeh al-Bukhari.*

Ad-Dakheel, Sa'eed Fa'iz. *Mawsu'atu Fiqhi A'isha Umm al-Mu'minin Hayatuha Wa Fiqhuha*. Dar an-Nafaes.

Adh-Dhahabi, Shamsuddin Muhammad. *Siyar A'lam an-Nubala*. 11th edition. Beirut: Mu'assisah al-Risalah, 1996.

Al-Jameel, Muhammad al-Faris. *Buyut an-Nabi wa Hujuratuha*. Beirut: Jadawel, 2016.

Al-Zarkashi, Badr al-Din. *Al-Ijāba li-Īrādi mā Istadraktahu 'Ā'isha 'Ala al-Sahābah*. Edited by Muhammad Binyamin Arul. Resalah Publishers, 1956; edited edition 2004.

Ibn Hajar al-Asqalani. *Fathul Bari Sharh Saheeh al-Bukhari*. Riyadh: Darussalam Publishers.

Mizzī, Yūsuf ibn al-Zakī 'Abd al-Rahmān. *Tahdhib al-Kamal fi Asma' al-Rijal*. Riyadh: Mu'assasat al-Risalah, 1985.

Muslim, Ibn al-Hajjaj. *Saheeh Muslim*.

Various Imams & Scholars. *Mawsu'ah al-Hadith ash-Sharif Al-Kutub As-Sittah*. Riyadh: Darussalam, 1999.

About the Author

Fatima Barkatulla is a British *Alimah* (Islamic scholar), author, and broadcaster. Growing up in London, she loved reading stories from the Quran, was fascinated by ancient Egypt, and dreamed of becoming an astronaut.

Her desire to understand the words of Allah directly, took her to Egypt to study the Shari'ah and the Arabic language. Fatima graduated from two Islamic seminaries in the UK with licences in Islamic Scholarship (*Shahadah 'Alimiyyah*) and holds an award-winning Master's Degree in Islamic Law from the School of Oriental and African Studies (SOAS), University of London, as well as a diploma in English Law from King's College London. She shares her knowledge through books, lectures, and more at *fatimabarkatulla.com.*

Fatima lives in London with her husband and four children. In her free time, she practises classical English calligraphy, visits historical sites, and is always partial to joining friends for a spot of cream tea. Her first book, *Khadijah: Islam's First Lady*, was also published by Learning Roots.

We hope you thoroughly enjoyed this book.
At Learning Roots, we support parents and
educators raise great Muslim children.
For more stories and resources like
the story of Aisha, please visit:
LearningRoots.com

KHADĪJAH

THE STORY OF ISLAM'S FIRST LADY

Also written by the same author,

available at LearningRoots.com

LEARNING
ROOTS.com

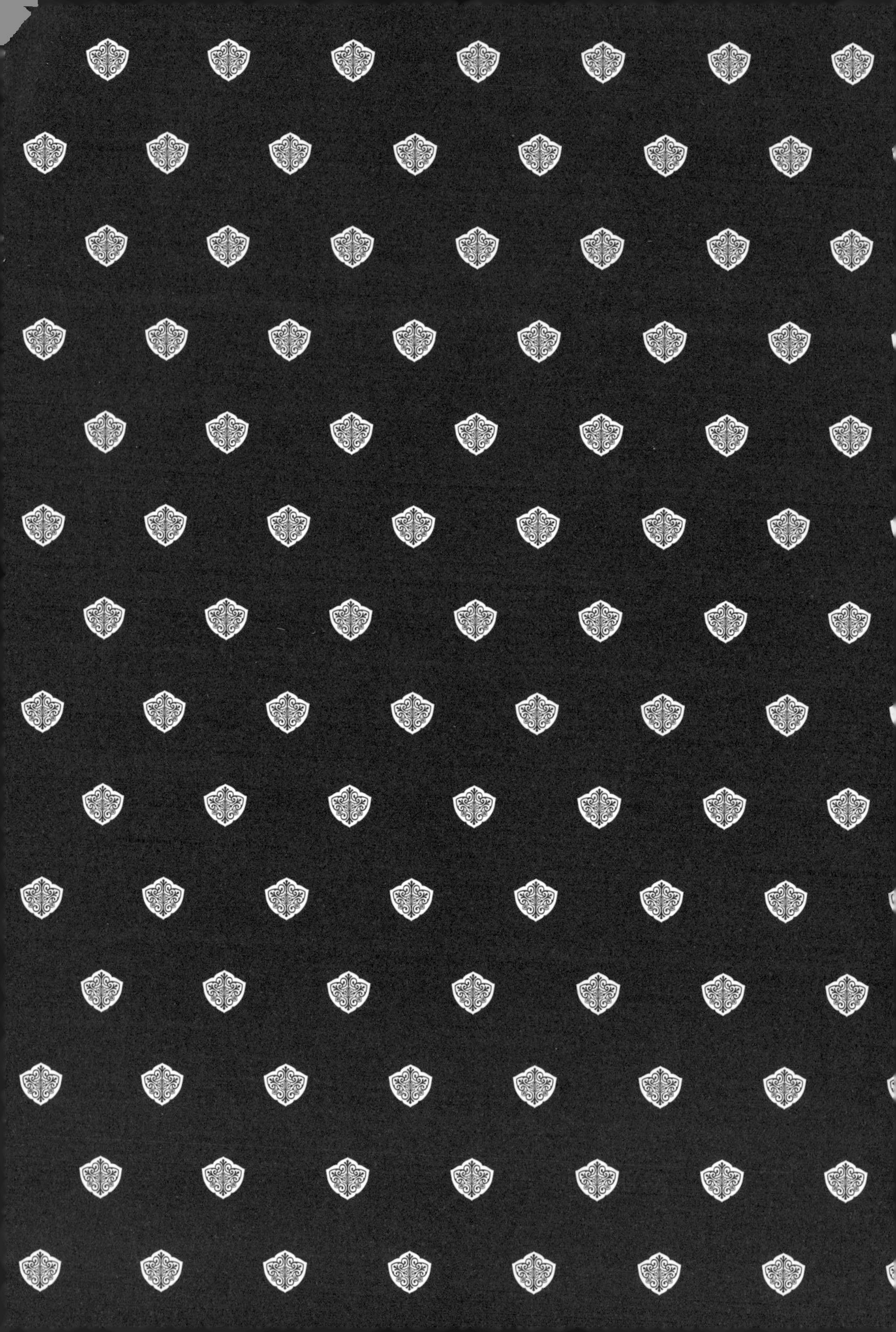